LIGHT ON AGING

AND

DYING

LIGHT ON AGING AND DYING

WISE WORDS SELECTED BY

Helen Nearing

A Harvest Book

Harcourt Brace & Company

San Diego   New York   London

Copyright © 1995 by Helen Nearing

Requests for permission to make copies of any part of the
work should be mailed to:
Permissions Department, Harcourt Brace & Company,
6277 Sea Harbor Drive, Orlando, Florida 32887-6777

This Harvest edition published by arrangement with
Tilbury House, Publishers, Gardiner, Maine.

Library of Congress Cataloging-in-Publication Data
Light on aging and dying/wise words selected by Helen Nearing.
p. cm.
Originally published: Gardiner, Me.: Tilbury House, c1995.
ISBN 0-15-600496-8
1. Old age—Quotations, maxims, etc.
2. Death—Quotations, maxims, etc. I. Nearing, Helen.
PN6084.O5L54
305.26—dc21 97-20613

Text set in Perpetua
Design by Edith Allard
Printed in the United States of America

First Harvest edition 1997
A C E F D B

The permission acknowledgments found on page 148
constitute a continuation of the copyright page.

~~~ CONTENTS ~~~

FOREWORD

There is much speculation about life after death. What about life before death? To learn how to be old is one of life's last lessons. To learn how to die is the very last lesson of all.

When vital powers ebb and we realize we are on the downturn, we can prepare with equanimity or with trepidation. How we approach old age, and finally death, is our own affair and no one else's. We are the ones who must choose our attitudes and behavior.

Our live's experiences, well assimilated, can be our gift to the mainstream. We can take care to pass on in some form what we have learned in living our lives. We have received; now we can confer what we have learned and gained, while we are still around to do it. Up to the last moment of life there are opportunities to make a contributory mark.

The inevitable aging of the body need not cut us off from leading a good life. Even abed or in a wheelchair we can contribute in some slight or great way by little particulars of personal conduct. We can deal with circumstances in non-destructive ways: we can be pleasant and cheerful or we can growl and complain and criticize, demeaning others and their projects. While losing some of our vital powers, we can try to remain healthy and strong in mind and spirit, if not in body.

Psychological aging, melancholic and misanthropic, need not accompany physiological aging. There can be such a thing as successful aging. A sense of wholeness, of integrity, can be the culmination of old age. It can be a time of rich involvement, with a golden glow over the inevitable ending.

The whole of our lives so far has been our message. What now, in the time still available? We can deepen our awareness; we can fulfill ourselves and help others by imparting what we may have learned from the high and low phases of our existence. In that way we can find completion at the end of our lives.

It is here and now that we make the conditions of any future life. It does not matter much if we continue as our present personal entities. More important is what we have learned and what we have contributed to the general welfare. The more aware we become, the more we participate productively, the more lessons we can learn—the more we enhance the whole.

A good old age can be the crown of all of our life's experiences, the masterwork of a lifetime. Behind us are years of actions and thoughts that developed us, changed us—and the world—for the better or the worse. We know in our inner selves which they have been and to what goal they have led.

That is past and gone. Now, or at any age, we can still make adjustments, can still become the best of what was in embryo at our birth. We came with incalculable opportunities ahead, no matter in what circumstances we were born. Some changes for the better we grasped; others we let slip. We sometimes frittered away our time and got nowhere; at other times we made the very most of the situations in which we found ourselves. It is up to us still to become what we are capable of becoming. There is time while we are still in the body.

Eastern philosophies and religions hold that the first part of life is for learning; the second, for household duties and social service; with the last part for one's higher self, for spiritual growth, for abstract thought and reflection. A long and healthy old age grants time for such a transition and preparation for dying, for graduation and the freedom that graduation brings. The episode of dying marks the close of one chapter of living, the relinquishment of earthly activities, the way on to the way out, the door to the onward way.

Dying is a process, with death as the destination—the greatest adventure of all. Why not look forward to it and prepare happily for it?

It is told of an old English laborer that he asked on his deathbed for his spade and fork to be placed close to his couch. "I'm 'avin' 'em in me coffin. I don't rightly know what they'll be settin' me to over there." He wanted to be prepared and he was.

Just as the last stages of one's life can be a shiningness or shadowed, so the act of dying can be bright or dark. It can be a harrowing ordeal or a hallowed happening. As we can live into our old age with consideration and grace, we can approach death with minimal distress, meeting it with dignity and deference.

There are techniques for dying well, just as there are for living well. There are ways of transition, sane approaches to death. We can make a conscious and worthy exit. Dying can be a natural and desirable process, a happy act, a rendering back to the whole what has been separated for a time—a willing and glad restitution, almost a celebration of successful aging.

*   *   *

When I was nearly ninety, among the countless visitors who came to our Forest Farm was a little girl with her parents. She listened to the appreciative comments on my great age and watched me as I moved easily around the house and garden. Before they left, she handed me a paper on which she had made a crayon drawing "To Helen," with pine trees in the foreground, two little flying birds, some notes of music they were singing, and the words: "89 ISN'T SO BAD." It is possible she may remember that when she becomes my age.

Being ninety-one at this writing, I have lived long and healthily and happily to this aged present. Now, in the not too distant future, I can look forward expectantly to release from the body that has served me so well for so long. Life has come almost full circle and I am ready to go on.

In the universal life that flows around us, any notion of death as a final end or a complete cessation is, to my mind, untenable. There is birth and there is death. They are more nearly two events in a whole life of livingness—with youth, maturity and old age, diversions in between—familiar features of human existence. Life links them all and continues beyond.

Is there a permanent ageless "I" that survives through a greater cycle? In a sense, who and what we are has no age. There seems to be a center of consciousness in each entity that is separate from the body. How long does that exist after the body dies? What awaits it?

But we have a job to do first—we must live until death. Years, days, hours, or minutes lie ahead. What will our life before death and at death be like?

In *The Tibetan Book of the Dead* those who are dying are called "the triumphant." In certain parts of ancient Japan, old people who sensed their end approaching went out into the mountains to die there alone. Eskimos are known to have done the same in the solitude of their snows. These were conscious exits—a leaving of life voluntarily——a sort of death-management and control.

My husband, Scott Nearing, died with deliberation and in full consciousness. He knew exactly what he was doing and planned it in advance. It was a death in keeping with his life—a reasoned process which he wanted to experience and make manifest. Death, to him, was merely the last stage in his growth, a natural organic act. He knew he was near the end and he wanted a death by choice——his own decision. His life had been sane and lived quietly and purposively. He wanted to go the same way——to live right into death.

One day, as we were starting our evening meal at the table, he said, "I think I won't eat any more." He was ninety-nine, approaching his hundredth year. His body was wearing out, his usual vigor ebbing, and he was ready to call it quits. He thought he had lived long enough, and he was interested to know what lay beyond. He believed in some kind of survival of the spirit, some continuity, and was ready to enter into and partake of that phase, as he had learned from and contributed to the physical phases of life.

From that time——a month before his hundredth birthday——he abstained from all solid food, taking only liquids. He waned and lost his strength, but kept his wits and good cheer—and determination. After a month of fasting on vegetable and fruit juices he announced, "Only water, please."

His aim had been to avoid all pills, drugs, doctors, and particularly forced feeding in hospitals or nursing homes. He had wanted to die at home, quietly, and in his own good time. All of which he did, simply and serenely and resolutely. He stepped quietly and consciously into death.

At the very end, alone with me, after a week on water, he

breathed his last, detached and yet still aware. He drifted away and off, like an autumn leaf from the parent tree, effortlessly and tranquilly. It was a benign and calm departure—well-timed and appropriate. He breathed low; then he breathed no more. He went somewhere else, with active volition. He had practiced the art of dying well.

Witnessing his purposive and voluntary ending, I felt impelled to get it down in writing and wrote the book *Loving and Leaving the Good Life* as a memoir to him. This led me to much reading on the subject of death and dying and to utilizing my fifty or more years' collection of hundreds of apt quotations on the topic from ancient and contemporary writers.

Hence this book. I offer it in the hope that from among the readers there will be those to whom the varied words will be as they are to me, an illumination and inspiration. To my mind they are too good to lose. Men have speculated through the ages on our eventual destiny. Can we not learn from their thoughts and theories? Good sayings are pearls strung together. They should be treasured and passed on.

Emerson wrote in his *Celebration of Intellect*, "It were a good rule to read some lines at least every day that shall not be of the day's creation or task, but of a study for eternity."

—HKN

It has not always been possible to track a quotation to earth with all the details as to date and source. The author has made diligent efforts. If there are omissions, it is not for lack of trying.

Do all things end at death? Is there an imaginable afterlife?
Whither do we go and what becomes of us? What awaits us on
the other side of the frail illusion we call life? At the moment
when our heart stops beating, does matter triumph, or mind?
Does endless darkness or eternal light begin?

MAURICE MAETERLINCK   *The Measure of the Hours*   1907

LIGHT ON AGING

AND

DYING

I

GOOD
OLD AGE

*I want to tell people approaching and perhaps fearing age
that it is a time of discovery. If they say "Of what?" I can
only answer "We must find out for ourselves, otherwise it
won't be discovery."*

FLORIDA SCOTT-MAXWELL   *The Measure of My Days*   1968

Old age is one of the most unexpected of all things that happen to man.

LEON TROTSKY   *Diary in Exile*   1929

Every man desires to live long, but no one would be old.

JONATHAN SWIFT   *Miscellanies*   1740

Few people know how to be old.

FRANÇOIS DE LA ROCHEFAUCAULD   1664

I am old, yet I look at wise men and see that I am very young. I look over those stars yonder, and into the myriads of the aspirant and ordered souls, and see I am a stranger and a youth and have yet my spurs to win. Too ridiculous are these airs of age.

RALPH WALDO EMERSON   *Journal*   1847

I quite love my present age [he was 56]—the compensations, the advantages of it—the simplifications of freedom, independence,

memories. But I don't keep it long enough.
It passes too quickly.

<small>HENRY JAMES</small>   (remark to a young woman)   1899

In my old age there is a coming into flower. My
body wanes; my mind waxes.

<small>VICTOR HUGO</small>   (in a letter)   January 7, 1869

Anyone who stops learning is old, whether 20 or
80. Anyone who keeps learning stays young. The
greatest thing in life is to keep your mind young.

<small>HENRY FORD</small>   1940

In spite of illness, in spite even of the archenemy,
sorrow, one can remain alive long past the usual
date of disintegration if one is unafraid of change,
insatiable in intellectual curiosity, interested in big
things, and happy in small ways.

<small>EDITH WHARTON</small>

We who are old know that age is more than a disability. It is an intense and varied experience, almost beyond our capacity at times, but something to be carried high.

FLORIDA SCOTT-MAXWELL

The Measure of My Days   1968

I want to be thoroughly used up when I die, for the harder I work the more I live. I rejoice in life for its own sake. Life is no brief candle to me. It is a sort of splendid torch which I've got to hold up for the moment, and I want to make it burn as brightly as possible before handing it on to future generations.

GEORGE BERNARD SHAW   *Art and Public Money*   1907

Development can indeed continue beyond childhood and youth, beyond the seventies. It can continue until the very end of life, given purposes that challenge and use our human abilities.... In sum, our development does not necessarily end at any age. We can continue to develop in our eighties, even to our nineties.

BETTY FRIEDAN   *The Fountain of Age*   1993

Michaelangelo did some of his best painting when past 80; Goethe wrote when past 80; Edison was still inventing at 92.... Frank Lloyd Wright at 90 was considered the most creative architect; Shaw was still writing plays at 90; Grandma Moses began painting at 79, etc., etc.

DR. MAXWELL NALTZ   *Psycho-Cybernetics*   1966

A person of sixty can grow as much as a child of six. The later years are a time for self-development, emancipation, a spiritual growth.

GAY GAER LUCE   *Your Second Life*   1979

Do not grow old, no matter how long you live. Never cease to stand like curious children before the Great Mystery into which we are born.

ALBERT EINSTEIN   *The Human Side*

As I approve of a Youth that has something of the Old Man in him, so I am no less pleased with an Old Man that has something of the Youth.

CICERO

As I go on in life, day by day, I become more of a
bewildered child; I cannot get used to this world, to
procreation, to heredity, to sight, to hearing.... I
could wish my days to be bound each to end by the
same open-mouthed wonder.

Robert Louis Stevenson
(letter to R.A.M. Stevenson)   1894

If I had influence with the good fairy who is
supposed to preside over the christening of all
children, I would ask that her gift to each child in
the world be a sense of wonder so indestructible
that it would last throughout life, as an unfailing
antidote against the boredom and disenchantment
of later years, the sterile preoccupation with things
that are artificial, the alienation from the sources of
our strength.

Rachel Carson   *The Silent Spring*   1962

There is real beauty to be found in knowing
that your end is going to catch up with you
faster than you expected, and that you have to

get all your living and laughing and crying done
as soon as you can.

LYN HELTON   *Soon There Will Be No More Me*   1972

Too many among us have been waylaid by age and
surprised by Time, ready to resign, to submit, to
surrender to the myth of "old age".... It cannot be
too often repeated that the growing old of the body
does not mean that the spirit has to grow old too.
Our conception of old age is a bad habit to which
most of us have been conditioned too early.

ASHLEY MONTAGU   *Growing Young*   1981

Ideally, every human being ought to live each
passing moment of his life as if the next moment
were going to be his last. He ought to be able to live
in the constant expectation of immediate death, and
to live like this, not morbidly but serenely.... The
closer that a human being can come to attaining this
ideal state of mind, the better and happier he and
she will be.

ARNOLD TOYNBEE   *Man's Concern With Death*   1968

Every moment is a golden one for him who has the vision to recognize it as such. Life is now, every moment, no matter if the world be full of death.

HENRY MILLER   *The World of Sex*   1957

There is only one way to get ready for immortality, and that is to live this life and live it as bravely and faithfully, and cheerfully as we can.

HENRY VAN DYKE

If the day and the night are such that you greet them with joy, and life emits a fragrance like flowers and sweet-scented herbs, is more elastic, more starry, more immortal—that is your success.... You must make tracks into the unknown. That is what you have your board and clothes for.

HENRY DAVID THOREAU   *Walden*   1854

The essence of the whole situation is to have in one's heart the romance of pilgrimage, to expect experience, both sweet and bitter, to desire the goal more than the prize; and to find the jewels of

patience, hopefulness, and wisdom by the way,
where one least expected to find them.

ARTHUR CHRISTOPHER BENSON

Beside Still Waters 1907

The soul, no longer having any great commerce
with the body, burgeons and comes into full flower.

SENECA

Life can be lived so miraculously on any scale in any
clime, under any condition.... Keep the miracle
alive. Live always in the miracle; make the miracle
more and more miraculous; swear allegiance to
nothing but live only miraculously; think only
miraculously; die miraculously. It matters little
how much is destroyed if only the germ of the
miraculous be preserved and nurtured.

HENRY MILLER *The Colossus of Maroussi* 1941

In the concentration camps, for example, in this
living laboratory and on this testing ground we
watched and witnessed some of our comrades
behave like swine while others behaved like saints.

Man has both potentialities within himself; which one is actualized depends on decisions but not on conditions.... The way in which a man accepts his fate and all the suffering it entails, the way in which he takes up his cross, gives him ample opportunity— even under the most difficult circumstances—to add a deeper meaning to his life. It may remain brave, dignified and unselfish.... His unique opportunity lies in the way in which he bears his burden.

VIKTOR E. FRANKL

Death Camp to Existentialism   1946

The greater part of our happiness depends on our dispositions and not on our circumstances.

MARTHA WASHINGTON   1800

Through our actions, we will create a new image of age—free and joyous, living with pain, saying what we really think and feel at last—knowing more than we ever knew we knew, not afraid of what anyone thinks of us anymore, moving with wonder into that unknown future we have helped shape for the generations coming after us.

BETTY FRIEDAN   *The Fountain of Age*   1993

What remains to me of strength becomes more precious for what is lost. I have lost one ear, but was never so alive to sweet sounds as now. My sight is so far impaired that the brightness in which nature was revealed to me in my youth is dimmed, but I never looked on nature with such pure joy as now. My limbs soon tire, but I never felt it such a privilege to move about in the open air, under the sky in sight of the infinity of creation, as at this moment. I almost think that my simple food, eaten by rule, was never relished so well. I am grateful then for my earthly tabernacle, though it does creak and shake not a little.

WILLIAM ELLERY CHANNING

(in a letter to Lucy Aikin)   1840

Winter is on my head, but eternal spring is in my heart. The nearer I approach the end, the plainer I hear around me the immortal symphonies of the worlds which invite me.... For half a century I have been writing thoughts in prose, verse, history, drama, romance, tradition, satire, ode, and song. I have tried them all, but I feel I have not said a thousandth part of that which is within me. When I go down to the grave, I can say "I have finished my day's work," but I cannot say "I have finished my life's work."

<small>Victor Hugo</small>   1880

When Goya was 80 he drew an ancient man propped on two sticks, with a great mass of white hair and beard all over his face, and the inscription "I am still learning."

<small>Simone de Beauvoir</small>   *Old Age*   1972

I intend to go on with my life by living it, not by buying into some notion that I no longer have the potential to become still better. I refuse to take seriously society's idea that at the arbitrary age of 65 I am suddenly a lamp going out.

<small>Roger S. Mills</small>

(quoting an elder in *History of Elder Hostel*)   1993

Our concept that a man has a useful life span of just so many years, and that on his sixtieth birthday, or sixty-second, or sixty-fifth, or whatever it may be, his productive capacity suddenly comes to an end, is a monstrous and inhuman concept. We must be flexible in our response to the gradually declining productivity of the aging, and recognize that there also comes with age a gradually increasing capacity to contribute to society.

ABRAHAM KAPLAN   *Love…and Death*   1973

Diogenes, when told to rest because he was growing old, said: "If I were running in the stadium, ought I to slacken my pace when approaching the goal? Ought I not rather to put on speed?"

Youth is not a time of life—it is a state of mind. Nobody grows old by merely living a number of years; people grow old by deserting their ideals. Years may wrinkle your skin, but to give up enthusiasm wrinkles the soul. You are as young as your faith, as old as your doubts; as young as your self-confidence, as old as your fear; as young as your hope, as old as your despair. In the central place of your heart there is a recording chamber; so long as it receives messages of beauty, hope, cheer, and courage—so long are you young. When the wires are all down and your heart is covered with the

snow of pessimism and the ice of cynicism, then—
and then only—are you grown old.

DOUGLAS MACARTHUR

Credo (quoting the essay "Youth," by Samuel Ullman)   1955

The name of death was never terrible to hear for
him that knew how to live.

BEAUMONT AND FLETCHER   *The Double Marriage*   1679

If we face now the reality, at 63 or 70, 75, 80, or
90, that we will indeed, sooner or later, die, then
the only big question is how are we going to live the
years we have left, however many or few they be?
What adventures can we now set out on to make
sure we'll be alive when we die? Can age itself be
such an adventure?

ANATOLE BROYARD

(article in *New York Times*)   April 1990

Don't waste life in doubts and fears; spend yourself
on the work before you, well assured that the right
performance of this hour's duties will be the best
preparation for the hours or ages that follow it.

RALPH WALDO EMERSON   "Immortality"   1885

The life which like the sun grows larger at its setting is the ideal.

WALTER M. BORTZ

We Live Too Short and Die Too Young   1991

Life need not unravel, stitch by stitch, like a strayed piece of knitting, leaving nothing but meaningless strands of wool in the old person's hands.

SIMONE DE BEAUVOIR   *Old Age*   1972

Is life so wretched? Isn't it rather your hands which are too small, your vision which is muddied? You are the one who must grow up.

DAG HAMMARSKJÖLD   *Markings*   1964

To die unchanged, except in body, is to have lived in vain.

HUGH L'ANSON FAUSSET   *Towards Fidelity*   1952

Fear not that thy life shall come to an end, but rather fear that it shall never have a beginning.

CARDINAL NEWMAN

If personal life has any real meaning at all, it points to a time when we shall grow into something of the measure of the stature of the fullness of a complete person, such as were the great representatives of the human race in other times and places.

Israel Martin   *The Nature of Eternal Life*   1976

Living is too much trouble unless one can get something big out of it.

Willa Cather   *The Song of the Lark*   1915

As time goes on, we grow older, and if we cannot find meaning and value in our later years, I think we betray the circumstance that our earlier years were also empty.

Abraham Kaplan   *Love...and Death*   1973

What is a man if the chief good and market of his time be but to sleep and feed?

Shakespeare   *Hamlet*

Hell begins on the day when God grants us a clear vision of all that we might have achieved, of all the gifts which we have wasted, of all that we might have done which we did not do.... For me the conception of Hell lies in two words: "too late."
GIAN-CARLO MENOTTI

Nothing can be more deplorable than to forego all the issues of living in a parlour with a regulated temperature.
ROBERT LOUIS STEVENSON   *Virginibus Puerisque*   1888

Do not pay too much attention to the stupid old body.... Quite lightly and decisively at each turning point in the path leave your body a little behind— with its hungers and sleeps, its funny little needs and vanities—paying no attention to them; stepping out at least a few steps in advance, absolutely determined not to be finally bound or weighed down by it.
EDWARD CARPENTER   *Towards Democracy*   1883

Do not let others impose upon you the mythology of "old age," for to feel young, even in many cases invigorated, is natural.... What is "old age" designed to be if not the fulfillment of childhood promises, the fullest expression of...youthfulness? The later years can be the happiest of one's life.

ASHLEY MONTAGU   *Growing Young*   1981

It is a tragedy that most of us die before we have begun to live.

ERICH FROMM

I have no intention of dying as long as I can do things. And if I do things there is no need to die. So I will live a long time.

ALBERT SCHWEITZER   (in a talk to his staff)

No man need fear death, because the ultimate tragedy of life is not death. The ultimate tragedy of life is not having lived fully when one is alive.

NORMAN COUSINS   *The Anatomy of An Illness*   1971

Granted that I must die, how shall I live? That is the fundamental human question.

MICHAEL NOVAK   *The Experience of Nothingness*

No one lives all the life of which he was capable. Our whole duty may be to clarify and increase what we are, to make our consciousness a finer quality. The effort of one's entire life would be needed if we are to return laden to our source.

FLORIDA SCOTT-MAXWELL

The Measure of My Days   1968

We are all guilty of crime—of the great crime of not living life to the full. But we are all potentially free. We can stop thinking of what we have failed to do and do whatever lies within our power. What these powers that are in us may be, no one has truly dared to imagine.

HENRY MILLER   *Sexus*   1949

We live horizontally. We do not live vertically, probing deep and aspiring high in our unconscious.

LOUIS ANSPACHER   *Challenge of the Unknown*   1947

It is not length of life, but depth of life.

RALPH WALDO EMERSON   "Immortality"   1885

A long life may not be good enough, but a good life is long enough.

BENJAMIN FRANKLIN

The fullness of years is not to be measured only in their number, but in the fullness of the days, and of the hours, in the fulfillments that were experienced.

ABRAHAM KAPLAN   *Love...and Death*   1973

I shall not waste my days trying to prolong them. I shall use my time.

JACK LONDON   (attributed)

A few years more or less matters little when set against the freedom and peace of mind one achieves the moment one stops running away from death.

SIMONE DE BEAUVOIR   *The Prime of Life*   1963

A positive experience of transience can release powerful forces which may act as an incentive for us to make the most of our remaining days.

ADOLPH LUCAS VISCHER   *On Growing Old*   1966

Wherever your life ends, it is all there. The advantage of living is not measured by length, but by use; some men have lived long, and lived little; attend to it while you are in it. It lies in your will, not in the number of your years, for you to have lived enough.

MICHEL DE MONTAIGNE   *Essays*   1580

The wise man lives as long as he should, not as long as he can. We will think of life in terms of quality, not quantity. Life, if thou knowest how to use it, is long enough.

SENECA   *Epistulae Morales*   60 A.D.

As we grow older and draw nearer to physical death, we inevitably become more conscious of the transience of our life here and of the world to which we unduly clung.

HUGH L'ANSON FAUSSET   *Towards Fidelity*   1952

To those who have obtained some wisdom in the process of reaching old age, death often assumes meaning as the proper outcome of life. It is nature's way of assuring much life and constant renewal. Time and customs change but the elderly tire of changing; it is time for others to take over, and the elderly person is willing to pass quietly from the scene.

ARTHUR J. DEIKMAN   *The American Handbook of Psychiatry*

Duration is not a test of true or false. The day of the dragon-fly or the night of the Saturnid moth is not invalid simply because that phase in its life cycle is brief. Validity need have no relation to time, to duration, to continuity. It is on another plane, judged by other standards.

ANNE MORROW LINDBERGH   *Gift From the Sea*   1955

Whatever time is assigned to each to live, with that he ought to be content.... For a short period of life is long enough for living well and honorably, and if you should advance further, you need no more

grieve than farmers do when the loveliness of
springtime has passed, that summer and autumn
have come.

CICERO *De Finibus* 45 B.C.

Not only Nature but man's being has its seasons, its
sequence of spring, autumn, summer, and winter.

CHUANG TZU

From my own experience, I think it is good if a
merciful fate sets a reasonable limit to the length of
time we live.

SIGMUND FREUD (in a letter to Thomas Mann) 1955

The span of life vouchsafed us, three-score and ten,
is short enough, if the spirit gets too haughty and
wants to live forever; but on the other hand, it is
also long enough, if the spirit is a little humble....
Anyone who is wise and has lived long enough to
witness the changes of fashion and morals and
politics through the rise and fall of three generations
should be perfectly satisfied to rise from his seat and

go away saying "It was a good show" when the curtain falls.

LIN YUTANG   *The Importance of Living*   1937

To be 70 years young is sometimes far more cheerful and hopeful than to be 40 years old.

OLIVER WENDELL HOLMES

I think that the dying pray at the last, not "please," but "thank you," as a guest thanks his host at the door.

ANNIE DILLARD   *Pilgrim At Tinker Creek*   1975

Thanks in old age—thanks ere I go,
For health, the mid-day sun, the impalpable air—
for life, mere life.

WALT WHITMAN   *Leaves of Grass*   1892

The thing you are ripening toward is the fruit of your life. It will make you bright inside, no matter what you are outside. It is a shining thing.

STEWART EDWARD WHITE   *With Folded Wings*   1947

If a family has one old person in it, it possesses
a jewel.

CHINESE PROVERB

Let not old age disgrace my high desire,
O heavenly soul, in human shape contain'd.
Old wood inflamed doth yield the bravest fire,
When younger doth in smoke his virtue spend.
Nor let white hairs, which on my face do grow,
Seem to your eyes of a disgraceful hue,
Since whiteness doth present the sweetest show,
Which makes all eyes do homage unto you.
Old age is wise and full of constant truth;
Old age well stay'd from ranging humour gives;
Old age hath known whatever was in youth;
Old age o'ercome, the greater honour gives.
And to old age, since you yourself aspire,
Let not old age disgrace my high desire.

SIR PHILIP SIDNEY   1580

I have scaled the peak and found no shelter in fame's
bleak and barren height. Lead me, my Guide, before
the light fades, into the valley of quiet where life's
harvest mellows into golden wisdom.

RABINDRANATH TAGORE   *Stray Birds*   1917

If man were to live this life like a poem he would be able to look upon the sunset of his life as his happiest period, and instead of trying to postpone the much feared old age, be able to look forward to it, and gradually build up to it as the best and happiest period of his existence.

LIN YUTANG   *The Importance of Living*   1937

As life wanes, and all the turbulent passions calm, Then for the teeming, quietest, happiest days of all! WALT WHITMAN   *Leaves of Grass*   1892

The whole of life is a journey toward youthful old age, toward self-contemplation, love, gaiety, and, in a fundamental sense, the most gratifying time of our lives.... "Old age" should be a harvest time when the riches of life are reaped and enjoyed, while it continues to be a special period for self-development and expansion.

ASHLEY MONTAGU   *Growing Young*   1981

Grow old along with me! The best is yet to be, The last of life, for which the first was made. ROBERT BROWNING   "Rabbi Ben Ezra"   1880

Old age, especially and honorcd old age, has so
great authority that this is of more value than all
the pleasures of youth.

CICERO

Youth, large, lusty, loving—youth, full of grace and
    force—
Do you know that Old Age may come after you
    with equal grace, force, and fascination?

WALT WHITMAN   *Leaves of Grass*   1871

It is perhaps life's greatest accomplishment to live
to old age, maintaining one's wits, one's sense of
humor, one's health, and one's charm.

YEHUDI MENUHIN   *Unfinished Journey*   1981

Character makes flesh and blood comely and alive,
adorns wrinkles and old hair.

RALPH WALDO EMERSON   "Character"   1842

The wrinkled smile of completeness that follows
    a life
lived undaunted and unsoured with accepted lies.
If people lived without accepting lies
they would ripen like apples, and be scented like
    pippins
in their old age.
Soothing, old people should be, like apples
when one is tired of love.
Fragrant like yellowing leaves, and dim with the soft
stillness and satisfaction of autumn.

D.H. LAWRENCE   *Beautiful Old Age*

When grace combines with wrinkles, it is
admirable. There is an indescribable light of dawn
about intensely happy old age…The young man is
handsome, but the old, superb.

VICTOR HUGO   *Les Miserables*   1862

The Chinese have always pictured an old man with
ruddy cheeks and white hair as the symbol of
ultimate earthly happiness: their God of Longevity

with his high forehead, his ruddy face, his white beard—and how he smiles!

LIN YUTANG   *The Importance of Living*   1937

A healthy old Fellow, that is not a Fool, is the happiest creature living. It is at that time of Life only Men enjoy their faculties with pleasure and satisfaction. It is then we have nothing to manage, as the phrase is; we can speak the downright Truth, and whether the rest of the World will give us the privilege or not, we have so little to ask of them that we can take it.

SIR RICHARD STEELE   *The Tatler*   1709

It is really about time that age was accepted as part of life too.... We are afraid of growing old. And many of us spend more than half our waking hours trying to camouflage our age.... There is nothing more beautiful than an unadorned old face with the lines that tell a story, a story of a life that has been lived with some fullness.

HELEN HAYES   *A Gift of Joy*   1965

We must not forget that only a very few people are artists in life, that the art of life is the most distinguished and rarest of all the arts.

CARL G. JUNG   *Modern Man in Search of A Soul*   1933

Youth is a gift of nature; aging is a work of art.

ANONYMOUS

The goal of human life is constructing an architecture of the soul.

SIMONE WEIL   *La Connaisance Surnaturelle*

To compose our character is our duty, not to compose books, and to win, not battles and provinces, but order and tranquility in our conduct. Our great and glorious masterpiece is to live appropriately.

MICHEL DE MONTAIGNE   *Essays*   1580

The ordinary objects of human endeavor— property, outward success, luxury have always seemed to me contemptible. I have never looked upon ease and happiness as ends in themselves. Such an ethical basis I call more proper for a herd of swine. The ideals which have lighted me on my way and time after time given me new courage to face life cheerfully, have been Truth, Goodness, and Beauty.

ALBERT EINSTEIN   *The World As I See It*   1949

In the midst of all the doubts which have been discussed for 4,000 years in 4,000 ways, the safest course is to do nothing against one's conscience. With this secret, we can enjoy life and have no fear of death.

VOLTAIRE   (letter to Frederick the Great)   1767

We should lead decent human lives simply because we are decent human beings.... If one accepts the statement that doing good is its own justification, one cannot help regarding all theological baits to right living as redundant and tending to colour the luster of a moral truth. Love among men should be a final absolute fact. We should be able to look at each other and love each other without being reminded of a third party in heaven.

LIN YUTANG *The Importance of Living* 1937

The root of the matter is a very simple and old-fashioned thing, a thing so simple that I am almost ashamed to mention it for fear of the derisive smile with which cynics will greet my words. The thing I mean—please forgive me for mentioning it—is love, or compassion. If you feel this, you have a motive for existence, a reason for courage, a guide in action, an imperative necessity for intellectual honesty. If you feel this, you have all that anybody should need in the way of religion.

BERTRAND RUSSELL *The Impact of Science on Society* 1902

More and more I come to value charity and love of one's fellow beings above everything else.... All our lauded technological progress —our very civilization—is like the axe in the hand of the pathological criminal.

ALBERT EINSTEIN *The Human Side* 1979

One can have no happiness either in this world or the next but by extreme and vehement love.

Sir Kenelm Digby   1661

So long as we love, we serve; so long as we are loved by others, I would almost say we are indispensible.

Robert Louis Stevenson   *Lay Morals*

Memory sleeps, action sleeps, but love is awake. It does not think or plant or labour to remember, but it loves; it is withdrawn from the surface of life to the centre.

Father George Congreve

(to a 90-year-old contemporary)   1918

If you knew that you were going to die tonight, or merely that you would have to go away and never return, would you, looking upon men and things for the last time, see them in the same light that you have hitherto seen them? Would you not love as you never yet have loved?

Maurice Maeterlinck

The Treasure of the Humble   1918

The tragedy of life is not in the fact of death. The tragedy of life is in what dies inside a man while he lives—the death of genuine feeling, the death of inspired response; the death of awareness that makes it possible to feel the pain or the glory of other men in oneself.... No man need fear death: he need fear only that he may die without having known his greatest power—the power of his free will to give his life for others.

ALBERT SCHWEITZER   1958

We are not put here to bend all our efforts toward getting out of earthly life without living it and learning by our experiences. We are put here to live and love and grow and progress.

MAX FREEDOM LONG   *The Secret Science at Work*   1949

Do not seek death. Death will find you. But seek the road which makes death a fulfillment.

DAG HAMMARSKJÖLD   *Markings*   1964

The way to get the best out of life is to take care to use on all occasions all the intelligence, affection, and will we have.

ERNEST WOOD   *The Glorious Presence*   1951

In his own life a man is not to expect happiness, only to profit by it gladly when it shall arise. He is on duty here, he knows not how or why, and does not need to know; he knows not for what hire, and must not ask. Somehow or other, though he does not know what goodness is, he must try to be good; somehow or other, though he cannot tell what will do it, he must try to give happiness to others.

ROBERT LOUIS STEVENSON
"A Christmas Sermon"   1888

Do all the good you can
By all the means you can
In all the ways you can
In all the places you can
At all the times you can
To all the people you can
As long as ever you can.

JOHN WESLEY   *Journal*   1790

When you were born, you cried, and the whole world rejoiced. Live such a life that when you die the world will cry and you will rejoice.

ANONYMOUS

I have always been attracted by the idea of the Brahmans that a man should devote his youth to study, his maturity to the duties and responsibilities of a householder, and his age to study, abstract thought, and meditation on the Absolute.

W. SOMERSET MAUGHAM   *The Narrow Corner*   1952

The young should get instruction; grown men should practice doing good; and old men should withdraw from all civil and military occupations and live at their own discretion, without being tied down to fixed office.

SOCRATES

The first part of life is for learning. The second for service, and the last is for oneself. It is a time to discover inner richness and for self-development and spiritual growth. It is also a time of transition and preparation for dying. The closer we come to death, the closer we can come to reality and truth.

GAY GAER LUCE   *Your Second Life*   1979

It may be that a man can learn a little something useful by suffering the sense of dying, and even that the longer he attends its school the more he will learn both about the conduct of this life and the demeanor of its close. What is indicated on this hypothesis is a lifelong expectation of a conscious experience of death.

MILTON MAYER   *On Death*   1965

Without the awareness of death, one would be only an ordinary man involved in ordinary acts. One would lack the necessary potency, the necessary concentration that transforms one's ordinary time on earth into magical power.

CARLOS CASTANEDA   *A Separate Reality*   1971

Perhaps middle age is, or should be, a period of shedding shells, the shell of ambition, the shell of material accumulations and possessions, the shell of the ego,…one's pride, one's false ambitions, one's mask, one's armor. Was that armor not put on to protect one from the competitive world? If one ceases to compete, does one need it? Perhaps one can at last in middle age, if not earlier, be completely oneself. And what a liberation that would be!

ANNE MORROW LINDBERGH   *Gift From the Sea*   1955

In many ways, it is the old that are to be envied by the young; they have so much less to lose that often they are capable of much more dedication and commitment to the values, ideals, and principles which provide meaning to all our lives.

ABRAHAM KAPLAN   *Love…and Death*   1973

In the conduct of life let us, as age and infirmity steal on us, contentedly resign the front seat and games to these bright children, our better representatives, nor expect compliments or inquiries— much less, gifts or love any longer (which to expect is ridiculous) and, not at all wondering why our friends do not come to us (much more wondering when they do), decently withdraw ourselves into modest and solitary resignation and rest.

RALPH WALDO EMERSON   *Journal*   1849

I would be well content to entertain the lag-end of my life with quiet hours.

SHAKESPEARE   *Henry IV*

The evening of life brings with it its lamp.

JOSEPH JOUBERT   *Essays*   1842

There is the silence of age,
Too full of wisdom for the tongue to utter it
In words intelligible to those who have not lived
The great range of life.

EDGAR LEE MASTERS   *Silence*   1900

To have a beautiful old age, you must live a beautiful youth, for we ourselves are posterity, and every man is his own ancestor. I am today what I am because I was yesterday what I was.... We often

hear of the beauties of old age, but the only old age
that is beautiful is the one the man has been long
preparing for by living a beautiful life. Everyone of
us is right now preparing for old age.... There may
be a substitute somewhere in the world for Good
Nature, but I do not know where it can be found.
The secret of salvation is this: keep sweet, be useful,
and keep busy.

ELBERT HUBBARD   *Scrap Book*   1930

Let us be content, in work, to do the thing we can
and not presume to fret because it's little.

ELIZABETH BARRETT BROWNING   *Aurora Leigh*   1883

Sufficient to today are the duties of today. Don't
waste life in doubts and fears; spend yourself on the
work before you; well assured that the right
performance of this hour's duties will be the best
preparation for the hours or ages that follow it.
The name of death was never terrible to him that
knew how to live.

RALPH WALDO EMERSON   *Essays*   1883

To accomplish great things we must live as if we were never going to die.

Luc Clapiers   *Maxims*   1747

If you want immortality—make it.

Joaquin Miller   *A Song of Creation*   1913

Become what you really are.

Aldous Huxley   *Island*   1962

To be what we are, and to become what we are capable of becoming, is the only end of life.

Robert Louis Stevenson   *Men and Books*   1888

He who would be a great soul in future, must be a great soul now.

Ralph Waldo Emerson   *Conduct of Life*   1860

Whatever anyone has contributed during his life—
of creation, formation, or preservation—to the sum
of human idealism, is his immortal part.

GUSTAV FECHNER   *Life After Death*   1836

The sweetest Canticle is when a Man hath obtained
worthy ends and expectations.... A Mind fixt and
bent on somewhat that is good averts the Dolors of
Death. When a Man hath obtained worthy ends and
expectations Death openeth the Gate to good Fame,
and extinguisheth Ennuie.

SIR FRANCIS BACON   *Essays and Counsels*   1625

If we are indeed here to perfect and complete our
own natures and grow larger, stronger, for some
nobler career in the future, we had all best bestir
ourselves to the utmost while we have the time.

ROBERT LOUIS STEVENSON   *Crabbed Age & Youth*   1888

Nothing must be postponed; find eternity in
each moment.

HENRY DAVID THOREAU   *Walden*   1854

Parts of the aging process are scary, of course, but the more we know about them, the less they need be. That is why I wish we were more deliberately, in our early years, to prepare for this condition. It would leave a lot of us freed to enjoy the obvious rewards of being old.... What is important is that our dispassionate acceptance of attrition be matched by a full use of everything that has ever happened in all the long wonderful-ghastly years to free a person's mind from his body...to use the experience, both great and evil, so that physical annoyances are surmountable in an alert and even mirthful appreciation of life itself.

M.F.K. FISHER   *Sister Age*   1983

It is not worthy of a man to postpone his struggle with death until the moment when it arrives to carry him off.

JACQUES BOSSUET   *Oraisons Funebres*   1690

I should like to see some prospect of good to mankind. I should like to leave some sterling mark behind me. I should like to have some friendly hand

consign me to the grave. On these conditions I am
ready, if not willing, to depart.

WILLIAM HAZLITT   *Table Talk*   1812

Death hangs over thee. While thou still live, while
thou may, do good.

MARCUS AURELIUS   *Reflections*   180 A.D.

The only preparation for death that is of any real
use or importance is a well-spent life.

CHARLES WEBSTER LEADBEATER
The Other Side of Death   1920

Do not fear death so much, but rather the
inadequate life.

BERTOLT BRECHT

The greatest dignity to be found in death is the
dignity of the life that preceded it. Hope resides in
the meaning of what our lives have been.

SHERWIN NEULAND   *How We Die*   1994

Immortality will come to such as are fit for it, and he who would be a great soul in future must be a great soul now.

RALPH WALDO EMERSON   "Worship"   1841

The years seem to rush by now, and I think of death as a fast-approaching end of a journey. Double and treble reason for loving as well as working while it is day.

GEORGE ELIOT   (in a letter)   1861

The morning drum-call on my eager ear
Thrills unforgotten yet; the morning dew
Lies yet undried along my field of noon.
But now I pause a while in what I do,
And count the bell, and tremble lest I hear
(My work untrimmed) the sunset gun too soon.

ROBERT LOUIS STEVENSON   *Collected Poems*

We all wish to have, at the moment of departing from this life, as clean a bill of spiritual health as it may be possible for a human being to earn; and if we take this wish seriously, it will move us to keep our spiritual condition constantly under review.

ARNOLD TOYNBEE

"What Happens When You Die"   1968

You grow more selective towards the countless possibilities of life.... You ask yourself: What have I neglected? What should I cultivate more? What would be more meaningful? Which time was wasted and which could be used better? You watch less television and read more—fewer newspapers and more books.... Viewing life from the perspective of death, we are made freer. Seeing something for the last time is nearly as good as seeing it for the first time.

PETER NOLL   *In the Face of Death*   1987

Age is opportunity no less
Than youth itself, though in another dress,
And as the evening twilight fades away
The sky is filled with stars invisible by day.

HENRY WADSWORTH LONGFELLOW

"Morituri Salutamus"   1841

And now let us believe in a long year that is given to us: new, untouched, full of things that have never been, full of work that has never been done, full of tasks, claims, and demands—necessary, serious, and great things.

RAINER MARIA RILKE

There is only one solution if old age is not to be an absurd parody of our former life, and that is to go on pursuing ends that give existence meaning— devotion to individuals, to groups or causes, social, political, intellectual or creative work.

SIMONE DE BEAUVOIR   *Old Age*   1972

The aging need opportunities for a continuation of the creative work which, fundamentally, is essential to any significant human experience. It is not enough to kill time with what are called hobbies, to sit about, even in the sunshine and in the company of other aging people, doing nothing more significant than waiting for death. The aging must be given opportunity to continue, as long as there is breath within them, to serve the people and purposes, the causes, institutions, and enterprises which gave meaning to the whole course of their lives.

ABRAHAM KAPLAN   *Love...and Death*   1973

Work helps prevent one from getting old. My work is my life. I cannot think of one without the other. The man who works and is never bored, is never old. A person is not old until regrets take the place of hopes and plans. Work and interest in worthwhile things are the best remedy for aging.

SCOTT NEARING   (in conversation)   1980

I want a man to act, and to prolong the functions of life as long as he can; and I want death to find me planting my cabbages.

MICHEL DE MONTAIGNE   *Essays*   1580

Farm as if you would live forever, and live as if you would die tomorrow.

GEORGE HENDERSON   *The Farming Ladder*   1944

Good! A remedy without physician, gold or sorcery.
Away forthwith, and to the fields repair.
Begin to delve, to cultivate the ground.
Thy senses and thyself continue
Within the very narrowest round.
Support thyself upon the simplest fare.
Live like the very brute the brutes among.
Neither esteem it robbery
The acre thou dost reap, thyself to dung.
This is the best method, credit me,
Again at eighty, to grow hale and young.

GOETHE   *Faust*   1808

The old ship is not in a state to make many
voyages, but the flag is still at the mast and I am still
at the wheel.

WALT WHITMAN   *Leaves of Grass*   1892

As the bird trims herself to the gale,
I trim myself to the storm of time.
I man the rudder, reef the sail,
Obey the voice at eve obeyed at prime;
Lowly, faithful, banish fear,

Right onward drive unharmed;
The port, well worth the cruise, is near
And every wave is charmed.

RALPH WALDO EMERSON   "Terminus"   1870

Waves lift and fall, as well as move forward.... Accept the recession into the quiet hollow, into the slow-sucking trough, as part of the great rhythm— without which there would be stagnation. Learn to take it as the repose period, the gathering period, the period in which the mighty forces that lift the wave upward are quietly, powerfully coming in. If you could only feel this, visualize this, never again would you be uneasy, depressed, low-spirited, discouraged, merely because of the natural, inevitable, necessary ebb and flow.... Accept the quietude with your folded wings, knowing that it is the law, that soon beneath your breast the stir of gathering forces must be felt.

STEWART EDWARD WHITE   *With Folded Wings*   1947

The compensation of growing old is that the passions remain as strong as ever, but one has gained—at last!—the power which adds the supreme flavour to existence——the power of taking hold of experience, of turning it round, slowly in the light.

<small>VIRGINIA WOOLF</small>   *Mrs. Dalloway*   1926

A person spends years coming into his own, developing his talent, his unique gifts, perfecting his discriminations about the world, broadening and sharpening his appetite, learning to bear the disappointments of life, become mature, seasoned——finally a unique creature in nature, standing with some dignity and nobility and transcending the animal condition…and then he is good only for dying…. He has to go the way of the grasshopper, even though it takes longer…. Who knows what form the forward momentum of life will take in the time ahead, or what use it will make of our anguished searching? The most that any of us can seem to do is to fashion something——an object or ourselves——and drop it into the confusion, make an offering of it, so to speak, to the life force.

<small>ERNEST BECKER</small>   *The Denial of Death*   1973

The crown of life is neither happiness nor annihilation; it is understanding. These are the moments of revelation which compensate for the chaos, the discomfort, the toil of living.... These are the moments in which all the disorder of life assumes a pattern. We see; we understand; and immediately the intolerable burden becomes tolerable; we stand for a moment on the slopes of that great mountain from the summit of which we can see the truth, and thus enjoy the greatest felicity of which we are capable.

WINIFRED HOLTBY   *Virginia Woolf*   1978

Surely when the inevitable day shall arrive and the ineluctable hour of death shall come to dismiss the soul from this life, it shall profit us not to be pointed out...on the squares and at crowded crossings, to have been a king or a great prelate, to have abounded in wealth and influence and enjoyments, but only to have lived chastely, piously, and innocently.

PETRARCH   1360

Old age hath yet his honor and his toil.
Death closes all; but something ere the end,
Some work of noble note, may yet be done...

'Tis not too late to seek a newer world.
Push off, and sitting well in order, smite
The sounding furrows; for my purpose holds
To sail beyond the sunset, and the baths
Of all the western stars until I die...
Though much is taken, much abides, and though
We are not now that strength which in old days
Moved earth and heaven, that which we are, we are;
One equal temper of heroic hearts,
Made weak by time and fate, but strong in will
To strive, to seek, to find, and not to yield.

ALFRED LORD TENNYSON   "Ulysses"   1842

The year hastens to the close. What is it to me? That
I am 25 or 58 is as nothing. Should I mourn that the
spring flowers are gone, that the summer fruit has
ripened, that the harvest is reaped, that the snow
has fallen?

RALPH WALDO EMERSON   *Journal*   1831

You are old enough; you have given your message
to the world. If you go, it will not be an
inharmonious thing.

WILLIAM JAMES   (in a letter to his dying father)

There is nothing to be unhappy about the fact that we are, as it were, delivered upon this beautiful earth as its transient guests for a good part of a century.

LIN YUTANG   *The Importance of Living*   1937

A positive experience of transience can release powerful forces which may act as an incentive for us to make the most of our remaining days.

ADOLPH LUCAS VISCHER   *On Growing Old*   1966

Always consider human things as ephemeral. You were born yesterday, tomorrow your body may be embalmed or a cinder. Therefore spend the present moment according to nature and finish up your life with serenity, like a ripe olive that falls, blessing the earth which nourished it and giving thanks to the tree that bore it.

MARCUS AURELIUS   *Reflections*   180 A.D.

Let life ripen and then let it fall.

LAO TZU

No one can really stop growing old.... Since there is no use fighting against nature one might just as well end with a grand finale of peace and serenity and spiritual contentment and not with the crash of a broken drum or cracked cymbals.

LIN YUTANG   *The Importance of Living*   1937

Old age and death, I saw, were not, after all insuperable. With the thinning of the flame there was a lessening of the oil; the lamp cooled gradually to its extinction. Death was only a moment, a breath, on the lowered wick.

JOSEPH HERGESHEIMER   *An Old House*   1925

And so the body dies, not of death but of too much life. The pressure of the electric current in time wears out the lamp, and the lamp must be renewed. Life never tires or ages. Only the form grows old.

CHRISTMAS HUMPHRIES   *Karma and Rebirth*

Tolstoy's illness dried him up, burnt something out of him. Inwardly he seemed to become lighter, more transparent, more resigned. His eyes are still

keen, his glance piercing. He listens attentively
as though recalling something which he has
forgotten, or as though waiting for something new
and unknown.

MAXIM GORKY   *Reminiscences of Leo Tolstoy*   1920

And if he die? He for an hour has been
Alive, aware of what it is to be.
The high majestic hills, the shining sea
He has looked upon, and meadows of golden-green.
The stars in all their glory he has seen.
Love he has felt. This poor dust that is he
Was stirred with pulse of inward liberty,
And touched the extremes of hope and all between.
Can the small pain of death-beds, can the sting
Of parting from the accustomed haunts of earth
Make him forget the bounty of his birth,
And cancel out his grateful wondering
That he has known exultance and the worth
Of being himself a song the dark powers sing?

ARTHUR DAVISON FICKE   *Poems*   1926

Old age, calm, expanded, broad with the haughty
  breadth of the universe.
Old age, flowing free with the delicious nearby
  freedom of death.
Old age, superbly rising!
O welcome, ineffable grace of dying days!
Walt Whitman   *Leaves of Grass*   1892

In old age, wandering on a trail of beauty, lively
may I walk. It is finished in beauty.
Navajo Nightway Chant

Be with me, Beauty, for the fire is dying;...
Beauty, have pity, for the strong have power,
The rich their wealth, the beautiful their grace,
Summer of man its sunlight and its flower,
Spring-time of man all April in a face....
Let me have wisdom, Beauty, wisdom and passion,
Bread and the soul, rain where the summers parch.
Give me but these, and, though the darkness close
Even the night will blossom as the rose.
John Masefield   "On Growing Old"   1960

Those that find the way in the morning can gladly die in the evening.

(ANCIENT APHORISM)

The old are nearing the harbor, the holy evening of man's life.

ROBERT LOUIS STEVENSON   "I Lay Me Down"

I know that the day will come when my sight of this earth shall be lost, and life will take its leave in silence, drawing the last curtain over my eyes. Yet stars will watch at night, and morning rise as before, and hours heave like the sea waves casting up pleasures and pains. When I think of the end of my moments, the barrier of the moments breaks and I see by the light of death thy world with its careless treasures. Rare is the lowliest seat, rare is its meanest of lives.

RABINDRANATH TAGORE   *Gitanjali*   1912

The sun closing his benediction, sinks,
And the darkening air thrills
With a sense of the triumphing night—

Night with her train of stars
And her great gift of sleep.
So be my passing!
My task accomplished and the long day done,
My wages taken, and in my heart
Some late lark singing,
Let me be gathered to the quiet west,
The sundown splendid and serene,
Death.

WILLIAM ERNEST HENLEY
"In Memoriam Margaritae Sorori"   1888

I see in you the estuary that enlarges and spreads
itself grandly as it pours into the great sea.
WALT WHITMAN   "To Old Age"   1892

An individual's human existence should be like a
river—small at first, narrowly contained within its
bounds, and seeking passionately past boulders and
even waterfalls. Gradually the river grows wide, the
banks recede, the waters flow more quietly, and in
the end, without any visible break they become
merged in the sea and painlessly lose their
individual being.
BERTRAND RUSSELL   1956

I do not want to die until I have faithfully made the most of my talent and cultivated the seed that was placed in me—until the last small twig has grown…. Everyone who is vouchsaved life has the obligation of carrying out to the last item the plan laid down in him. Then he may go. Probably that is the point at which most people die.

KÄTHE KÖLLWITZ   *Diary*   1915

Each one of us is born for a specific reason and purpose, and each one of us will die when he or she has accomplished whatever was to be accomplished. The in-between depends on our own willingness to make the best of every day, or every moment, of every opportunity. The choice is always yours.

ELISABETH KÜBLER-ROSS

To Live Until We Say Goodbye   1978

I strove with none, for none was worth my strife.
Nature I loved, and next to Nature, Art.
I warmed both hands before the fire of life;
It sinks, and I am ready to depart.

WALTER SAVAGE LANDOR   1860

I run to death, and death meets me as fast;
And all my pleasures are as yesterday.
This is my play's last scene, here heavens appoint
My pilgrimage's last mile; and my race,
Idly yet quickly run, hath this last pace,
My span's last inch, my minute's latest point.

JOHN DONNE   *Holy Sonnets*   1615

Here is a test to find whether your mission on earth
is finished: If you're alive, it isn't.

RICHARD BACH   *The Reluctant Messiah*   1977

II

THE ART
OF DYING

*Death is as natural as life, and should be
sweet and graceful.*

RALPH WALDO EMERSON   *Journal*   1844

How a person dies reveals much about how he or
she lived.

Milton Lamask   *The Biographer's Craft*   1986

To die in such a way that death is a fitting end to
one's life is not an easy art.

Ilya Ehrenberg   (attributed, before his death)

The art of dying graciously is nowhere advertised,
in spite of the fact that its market potential is great.

Milton Mayer   *On Death*   1965

Death is the most universal and most inexorable of
the demands that is made on us human beings.

Albert Kaplan   *Love...and Death*   1973

The character of our life is the character of our
dying; both are part of one process.

Stanley Keleman   *Living Your Dying*   1974

A good death doth honor to a whole life.

PETRARCH   1304

It is the most supremely interesting moment in life,
the only one, in fact, when living seems life, and I
count it as the greatest good fortune to have these
few months so full of interest and instruction in the
knowledge of my approaching death. It is so simple
to one's own person as any fact of nature, the fall of
a leaf or the blooming of a rose, and I have a delicious consciousness, ever present, of wide spaces
close at hand, and whisperings of release in the air.

ALICE JAMES   (in a letter to her brother William)   1891

Dying must surely be placed high among the two or
three supreme human experiences.

THOMAS BELL   *In the Midst of Life*   1961

Manifestation is a vast field of experience. As I
have lived eagerly and fully, to the extent of my
powers, so I pass on gladly and hopefully. Death is
either a transition or an awakening. In either case it

is to be welcomed, like every other aspect of the life process.

SCOTT NEARING   Last testament   1983

The manner of death is more important than death itself. Fine dying is man's privilege, for that, man can control. We cannot influence death but we can influence the style of our departure.

CYRUS SULZBERGER   *My Brother Death*   1961

I have always believed that the moment of death is the norm and goal of life.

SIMONE WEIL   (in one of her last letters)

If even dying is to be made a social function, then, please, grant me the favor of sneaking out on tiptoe without disturbing the party.

DAG HAMMARSKJÖLD   *Markings*   1964

It is too bad that dying is the last thing we do, because it could teach us so much about living.

ROBERT M. HERHOLD
Learning to Die, Learning to Live   1976

Out of the very love one bears to life, one should wish death to be free, deliberate, and a matter neither of chance or surprise.

FRIEDERICH NIETZSCHE

Thus Spake Zarathustra   1882

It were a salutary thing for each of us to work out his idea of death in the light of his days and the strength of his intelligence and to stand by it.

MAURICE MAETERLINCK   *Our Eternity*   1913

Embrace your death.... Cherish your awareness of death as a gift from the universe.

BRIAN SWIMME   *The Universe Is A Green Dragon*   1984

It is rather a relief and disburthening of the mind...a holiday time...to forget the troubled dream of life.

WILLIAM HAZLITT   *Table Talk*   1821

My body, eh? Friend Death, how now?
Why all this tedious pomp of writ?

Thou hast reclaimed it sure and slow
For half a century, bit by bit.

HELEN HUNT JACKSON   *Habeas Corpus*   1885

There is no physical or metaphysical reason why the
advent of death should not be as salutary as that of
sleep.... A day will come when life, grown wiser,
will depart silently at its hour, knowing that it has
reached its term, even as it withdraws silently every
evening, knowing that its task is done.

MAURICE MAETERLINCK   *Our Eternity*   1913

Ideally, every human being ought to live each
passing moment of his life as if the next moment
were to be his last. He ought to be able to live in the
constant expectation of immediate death and to live
like this, not morbidly, but serenely.

ARNOLD TOYNBEE   *Man's Concern With Death*   1968

Come, lovely and soothing Death,
Undulate round the world, serenely arriving, arriving,
In the day, in the night, to all, to each,

Sooner, or later, delicate Death.
    Praised be the fathomless universe,
For life and joy, and for objects and knowledge curious,
And for love, sweet love—but praise! praise! praise!
For the sure-enwinding arms of cool-enfolding Death.
WALT WHITMAN   *Leaves of Grass*   1892

Look on each day as if it were your last, and each
unlooked-for hour will seem a boon.
HORACE   *Epistles*   15 B.C.

Since we live with death, we ought to think of it
while living. To settle accounts, to draw a balance, is
important and useful. The pastors should make it
clear that it can be anyone's turn next; that everyone's turn comes at some point; that to prepare
oneself is good.
PETER NOLL   *In the Face of Death*   1987

Like a projectile flying to its goal, life ends in death.
Even its ascent and its zenith are only steps and
means to this goal. We grant goal and purpose to the
ascent of life, why not death? For 20 years and more

the growing man is being prepared for the complete unfolding of his individual nature, why should not the older man prepare himself 20 years and more for his death?

CARL JUNG   *The Soul and Death*   1934

Let us remove death's strangeness; let us practice it; let us accustom ourselves to it.... It is uncertain where death awaits; let us await it everywhere. We must be always booted and ready to go, as far as it is in our power. To be ready to die frees us from all bondage and thralldom.

MICHEL DE MONTAIGNE   *Essays*   1580

A man has the right to decide how long he may usefully live.

MARGUERITE YOURCENAR   *Memoirs of Hadrian*   1954

As long as I grow, I desire to live; but when the principle of growth is arrested, then I would willingly be removed.

ELIZABETH BARRETT BROWNING
(in a letter to her sister)   1857

It may be that a man can learn a little something useful by suffering the sense of dying, and even that the longer he attends its school the more he will learn both about the conduct of this life and the demeanor of its close. What is indicated, on this hypothesis, is a lifelong expectation and a conscious expectation of death.... Death takes us down a peg or two and cuts us and our furnishings to size; probably not a bad thing for most of us, and maybe the best thing that ever happened to any of us. Who knows?

MILTON MAYER   *On Death*   1965

When you are dying and coming to life in each moment, would-be scientific predictions about what will happen after death are of little consequence. The whole glory of it is that we do not know.

ALAN WATTS   *The Wisdom of Insecurity*   1951

Who knows if this experience we call dying is not really living, and if living is not really dying? Who knows if to be alive is not really to die, and if dying does not count in the nether world as being alive?

EURIPIDES   454 B.C.

Death is not a beginning; death is not an end. Who knows when the end is reached? Death may be the beginning of life. How do I know that love of life is not a delusion after all? How do I know that he who dreads to die is as a child who has lost the way and cannot find his home? How do I know but that the dead repent of having previously clung to life?

CHUANG TZU   300 B.C.

The hour of departure has arrived, and we go our ways—I to die, and you to live. Which is better only God knows. Perhaps God in his kindness is taking my part and securing me the opportunity of ending my life not only in season but also in the way that is easiest.

SOCRATES   399 B.C.

Socrates on his last day said "I would not positively assert that I shall join the company of those good men who have already departed from this life, but I cherish a good hope." With what a joyful soberness and gravity did he move through experience, never losing his balance, but serenely judging all till the moment came for him to enter behind the veil of death; and this he did with the same imperturbable good humour, neither lingering nor hasting but with a tranquil confidence that life was beginning rather than ending.

ARTHUR CHRISTOPHER BENSON

Beside Still Waters   1907

He left a world he was weary of with the cool indifference you quit a dirty inn to continue your journey to a place you hope for better accommodation.

LADY MARY WORTLEY MONTAGUE

(letter)   July 11, 1759

A single summer grant me, great powers, and a single autumn for fully ripened song, that, sated with the sweetness of my playing, my heart may more willingly die.... Once I lived like the gods, and more is not needed.

F. HOLDERLIN   *To the Fates*   1798

It is very good to have been man. And so we may go forward together with laughter in our hearts, and peace, thankful for the past, and for our own courage.

Olaf Stapledon   *Last and First Men*   1930

I have no regret at having lived, for I have so conducted my life that I do not feel that I was born to no purpose. I cheerfully quit from life as if it were an inn, not a home; for Nature has given us a hostelry in which to sojourn, not to abide.

Cicero   *De Senectute*   45 B.C.

My mental faculties demand that I leave the "house" I have inhabited without regret and, as far as I am able, the place I have occupied in the scheme of things uncluttered.

Eileen D. Garrett   *Many Voices*   1968

Never did a man prepare to leave the world more utterly and completely, nor detach himself from it more universally, than I propose to do.

Michel de Montaigne   *Essays*   1580

I am as weary as it is natural to be after a hard-working life, and I think I have fairly earned my rest. The organic elements that have held together for so long are tending to fall apart. Who would wish them to remain forcibly connected any longer?

SIGMUND FREUD   (letter to Pfister)   1925

If I had my life to live over again, I would form the habit of nightly composing myself to thoughts of death. I would practise, as it were, the remembrance of death. There is not another practise which so intensifies life. Death, when it approaches, ought not to take one by surprise. It should be part of the full expectancy of life.

MURIEL SPARK   *Momento Mori*   1959

I want to die with a premonition of death a week beforehand, with my mind serenely unshaken and free from attachment to my body.

CHUANG FENG

For my part, I would like to die fully conscious that I am dying...slow enough to allow death to insinuate itself into my body and fully unfold, so as not to miss the ultimate experience, the passage.

MARGUERITE YOURCENAR   *With Open Eyes*   1980

There is a technique of dying just as there is of living.... Why not welcome transition? Learn to glory in experience, which is the gift of wise old age, and look forward to the Great Adventure that confronts you.

ALICE A. BAILEY   *A Treatise on White Magic*   1934

Now I am about to take my last voyage, a great leap into the dark.

THOMAS HOBBES   (on his deathbed)   1679

To die should be the most interesting journey of all the journeys a man can make.

JAN WILLEM VAN DE WETERING
The Japanese Corpse   1977

In this freeing for the forward journey there must, one would think, be a great sense of joy and satisfaction—even as there must be in the freeing of a May-fly from its water-bred pupa into the glory of air and sunshine. A strange joy in shelling of the old husks, and in getting rid of the accumulated rubbish of a lifetime. A thousand and one tiresome old infirmities and bonds of the body slip off and the ship of the soul departs with a strange thrill and quiver upon its endless cruise.

EDWARD CARPENTER

The Drama of Love and Death   1912

Die everyday. Be reborn again every day.

NIKOS KAZANTZAKIS   *Saviors of God*   1929

Any act you perform may be your last. The only thing that counts is that you perform your absolute best in anything you do, because it may very well be the last thing you do.... Is this the act that I would want if it were to be my final act on earth, is a question that will drop more pettiness and idiocy from your life than almost anything else.

DAVID COPELAND

"Opening to the Whispers of Power"   1992

Every morning make up thy mind to die. Every evening freshen thy mind in the thought of death. And let this be done without end. Thus will thy mind be prepared. When thy mind is always set on death, thy way through life will always be straight and simple. If one lives a day, let him perform a day's duty and die. If he lives a month, let him perform a month's duty and die. If he lives a year, let him perform a year's duty and die.

YOSHIDA SHOIN   *The Hagakara*   18th Century

Death is a process of at-one-ment.... Through death, a great at-one-ing process is carried forward. In the fall of a leaf and its consequent identification with the soil on which it falls, we have a tiny illustration of this great and eternal process of at-one-ing.

ALICE A. BAILEY   *Esoteric Healing*   1953

I have never doubted that we could rise, calmly, healthfully, naturally, into a sensuous perception as far richer and more satisfying than the best of our present level, as that best is beyond the perception of the dullard or the animal.

MARY JOHNSTON   *Added Space*   1936

Let life be beautiful like summer flowers and death
be like autumn leaves.

RABINDRANATH TAGORE   *Stray Birds*   1917

What a simple thing death is, just as simple as the
falling of an autumn leaf.

VINCENT VAN GOGH
(in a letter to his brother Theo)   1885

How beautiful this dead leaf, yellow and bright
red, a leaf from the autumn. So simple in its death,
so lovely, full of the beauty and vitality of the whole
tree and summer. Strange that it has not
withered.... Why do human beings die so
miserably?... Why don't they die—as beautifully as
this leaf?

J. KRISHNAMURTI   *Last Journal*   1987

When the leaves fall, the whole earth is a cemetery
pleasant to walk in.... How beautifully they go to
their graves! How gently lay themselves down and
turn to mould. They teach us how to die. One
wonders if the time will ever come when men, with
their boasted faith in immortality, will lie down as

gracefully and as ripe—with such an Indian-summer
serenity will shed their bodies.

H. D. Thoreau   "Fallen Leaves"   1862

When his hour for death had come,
[The chief] slowly rais'd himself from the bed on the
    floor,
Drew on his war-dress, shirt, leggings, and girdled
    the belt around his waist,
Call'd for vermillion paint (his looking glass was held
    before him),
Painted half his face and neck, his wrists, and back-
    hands,
Put the scalp-knife carefully in his belt—then lying
    down, resting a moment,
Rose again, half sitting, smiled, gave in silence his
    extended hand to each and all,
Sank faintly low to the floor (tightly grasping the
    tomahawk handle),
Fixing his look on wife and children to the last.

Walt Whitman   *Leaves of Grass*   1892

Sam Staples, who had been Thoreau's jailor long ago
when the poll tax went unpaid, called upon him in

March and reported to Emerson: "Never spent an hour with more satisfaction. Never saw a man dying with so much pleasure and peace." Less than two months before he died, [Thoreau] wrote in a dictated letter: "You ask particularly after my health. I suppose that I have not many months to live, but, of course, I know nothing about it. I may add that I am enjoying existence as much as ever, and regret nothing...." Some orthodox member of the family asked him if he had made his peace with God. Only Thoreau could have answered as he did, that he was not aware he and God had ever quarreled.... As consciousness faded, he sank down below the level of articulate thought into the depths of his being where he met again the point at which the path of civilization had branched fatally away from the path of nature. "Moose," he whispered, and "Indians."

JOSEPH WOOD KRUTCH   *H.D. Thoreau*   1948

When the act of our living has actually spent itself of its own momentum, then we enjoy dying.

H. M. KALLEN   *Freedom in the Modern World*   1928

To die quietly of old age would be to go there on foot.
VINCENT VAN GOGH   (in a letter to his brother Theo)

Men who have seen life and death as just an
unbroken continuum, the swinging of an eternal
pendulum, have been able to move as freely into
death as they walked through life. Socrates went to
the grave almost perplexed by his companions'
tears. Many of the Zen masters actually anticipated
their "final" hour, meeting it with equilibrium and
even laughter.
PHILIP KAPLEAU   *The Wheel of Death*   1971

How would you be buried? asked Criton of
Socrates, shortly before the latter's death. Just as
you please, replied the sage, If you can but catch me
and I not elude your pursuit.

As Roshi Taji, a contemporary Zen master
approached death, his senior disciples assembled at
his bedside. One of them, remembering the Roshi
was fond of a certain kind of cake, had spent half a

day searching the pastry shops of Tokyo for this confection which he now presented to Roshi Taji. With a wan smile the dying man accepted a piece of the cake and slowly began munching it. As he grew weaker his disciples inquired whether he had any final words for them. "Yes," the Roshi replied. The disciples leaned closer to catch his words of wisdom. "Please tell us!" "My, but this cake is delicious," and with that he died.

(SOURCE UNKNOWN)

I'm going where washing ain't done, nor churning nor sewing, and everything else will be just to my wishes—for where they don't eat, there's no washing of dishes. Don't mourn for me now, nor mourn for me never, for I'm going to do nothing forever & ever.

ON AN ANONYMOUS SERVING MAID'S TOMBSTONE   1860

Did thee ever think what a dull place Heaven must be if the popular notion of it is correct? A state of sheer spiritual laziness—nothing to do because everything is done—nobody to help—nobody to

pity—nobody to pray for—no employment but to
sing hymns!

JOHN GREENLEAF WHITTIER
(in a letter to Elisabeth Lloyd)   1860

A long, long sleep, a famous sleep
    That makes no show for dawn
By stretch of limb or stir of lid,
    An independent one.

Was ever idleness like this?
    Within a hut of stone
To bask the centuries away
    Nor once look up for noon?

EMILY DICKINSON   *Poems*   1890

Death seems to me so often a relief, a rendering
up of responsibility, a quitting of many vexatious
trifles.

RALPH WALDO EMERSON   *Journal*   1845

When John was dying, he was asked if he wanted a
priest. "Good heavens, no!" was his hearty reply....

As he faced death, a few hours before his passing, a friend who had many times discussed philosophy with him over the chessboard came to say farewell. Like a player who is giving checkmate, John remarked, "Soon perhaps I shall know some of the real answers to the eternal questions." The old merry twinkle was in his eyes as if he were saying to his friend "I'm still a move ahead of you."

(FROM THE INTRODUCTION TO JOHN TETTEMER'S *I Was A Monk*)   1951

If I should die,
And you should live,
And time should gurgle on,
And morn should beam,
And noon should burn,
As it has usual done;
If birds would build as early,
And bees as bustling go—
One might depart at option
From enterprise below!
'Tis sweet to know that stocks will stand
When we with daisies lie,
That commerce will continue,
And trades as briskly fly.

It makes the parting tranquil
And keeps the soul serene,
The gentlemen so sprightly
Conduct the pleasing scene.

EMILY DICKINSON   *Poems*   1890

Grieve not that I die young. Is it not well to pass
away ere life hath lost its brightness?

FLORA HASTINGS   *Swan Song*   1830

Rilke's friend, Frau Knoop, wrote him of her
daughter's last words shortly before she died: "Now
I shall dance!"

RAINER MARIA RILKE
(footnote to *Sonnets to Orpheus*)   1942

Go then, merrily, to heaven.

RICHARD BURTON   *The Anatomy of Melancholy*   1621

Count no man happy till he dies.

EURIPIDES   *The Trojan Women*   414 B.C.

Smile, Death, as you fasten the blades to my feet
    for me.
On, on let us skate past the sleeping willows dusted
    with snow;
Show me your face. Why, the eyes are kind!
And we will not speak of life or believe in it or
    remember it as we go.

CHARLOTTE NEW   *The Farmer's Bride*   1920

Death is the true and best friend of humanity...the
key which unlocks the door to our true state of
happiness.

MOZART   (in a letter to his father)

I do not commiserate—I congratulate you...
Has anyone supposed it lucky to be born?
I hasten to inform him or her it is just as lucky to
die, and I know it.

WALT WHITMAN   *Leaves of Grass*   1892

We are put on this earth to celebrate. You give it
everything you have. Everything. That includes your
death. The greatest thing you can do is possess your

own death so that when it comes it is given, not taken. Honor your own death. It is a sacrament.... Death renders life magnificent.... Death walks beside one, and so does whatever one's sense of God is, or the sublime.

SCOTT SYMONS   (interview in *The Idler*)   June 1989

Pity is for the living; envy is for the dead.

MARK TWAIN   (attributed)

It is the time to celebrate!
Now comes the great Peace, the great Rest!
There flies a line of herons, eternally seeking
    Spring:
They know their path; they know their way.
What, oh my soul, have you to fear?

C.F. MEYER   *Hussens Kerker*

This life is the crossing of a sea, where we meet in the same narrow ship. In death we reach the shore and go to our different worlds.

RABINDRANATH TAGORE   *Stray Birds*   1917

All human beings are like travelers floating down the eternal river of time, embarking at a certain point and disembarking again at another point in order to make room for others waiting below the river to come aboard.

LIN YUTANG   *The Importance of Living*   1937

Thou hast embarked, thou has made the voyage, thou art come to shore, get out.

MARCUS AURELIUS   *Meditations*   160 A.D.

There is a usefulness of time when a man should go, and not occupy too long the ground to which others have a right to advance.

THOMAS JEFFERSON
(in a letter to Benjamin Rush)   1811

Necessary, timely death.... The little clock that sends us on our way when our room becomes more valuable than our company.

CARL BONHORST   (in a letter)   July 1978

Every human death is ultimately for the good of
the group.

ROBERT S. MORISON   *The Last Poem*   1974

I am old; I am going to die.... I often think about
it. I am getting ready.... It is time for me to
disencumber the world.

VICTOR HUGO

Learn to live well, or fairly make your will;
You've play'd, and lov'd, and ate, and drank your fill.
Walk sober off, before a sprightlier Age
Comes titt'ring on, and shoves you from the stage.

ALEXANDER POPE   *Pastorals*   1709

Coming at its due time, when the organism has
given all it can give, death is the great minister of
orderly evolution.

GUSTAV GELEY

From the Unconscious to the Conscious   1918

Death is only Nature's remedy for over-crowding.

GEORGE BERNARD SHAW   (attributed)

The experience itself must be enormously
interesting. Talk about starting on a journey! What
must the longest sea voyage be, compared with this
one, with its wonderful vista, a vision, and voices
calling? And again, since it is an experience that all
must go through and that countless millions of our
fellows have gone through and are still continually
going through, for that very reason alone it has a
fascination; and one feels that had one the opportunity to avoid it one would hardly wish to do so.

EDWARD CARPENTER

The Drama of Love and Death   1912

Peace, my heart, let the time for the parting be sweet.
Let it not be a death but completeness.
Let love melt into memory and pain into songs.
Let the flight through the sky end in the folding of
  wings over the nest.
Let the last touch of your hand be gentle like the
  flower of the night.

Stand still, O Beautiful End, for a moment, and say
    your last words in silence.
I bow to you and hold up my lamp to light you on
    your way.
RABINDRANATH TAGORE   *The Gardner*   1945

Let us cross over the river and rest under the shade
of the trees.
STONEWALL JACKSON   (last words)   1863

Now the death hour comes and this day will I die.
O make my grave and make it a broad and a high
    one...
On the right side leave for me a little window open,
At which the swallows may fly in to tell me when
    the Spring comes,
And when, in fair May moons, the nightingales may
    sing.
ROMAIC BALLAD   ca 1842

When my hour is come
let no teardrop fall
And no darkness hover

Round me where I lie.
Let the vastness call
One who was its lover.
Let me breathe the sky.
A. E.   *Poems*   1919

If I die, leave the balcony open.
FEDERICO GARCIA LORCA   (last words)   1935

At the last, tenderly,
From the walls of the powerful fortressed house,
From the clasp of the knitted locks, from the keep
    of the well-closed doors,
Let me be wafted.
Let me glide noiselessly forth;
With the key of softness unlock the locks—with a
    whisper
Set ope the doors, O soul.
Tenderly—be not impatient,
(Strong is your hold, O mortal flesh,
Strong is your hold, O love.)
WALT WHITMAN   *Leaves of Grass*   1892

For myself, I do not need to look in terms of survival after death. I feel myself to be part of the known properties of the earth's family, and that is enough. One day, the breath I have been privileged to use will become again a part of the earth's family being.... If there is another place to catch up with the "breath," I hope it will be as challenging as it has been here; but if it does not exist, it is enough that I have lived.

Eileen D. Garrett   *Many Voices*   1968

As for death, if there is nothing beyond, then for nothingness I offer thanks; if another mode of existence, with the old worn-out husk of a body left behind, this floundering, muddled mind given a longer range and a new precision, then for that I likewise offer thanks.

Malcolm Muggeridge
"Half in Love With Death"   1970

So far as the creative individual goes, life and death are of equal value; it is all a question of counterpoint. What is of vital concern, however, is how and where one meets life—or death. Life can be more deadly than death, and death on the other hand, can open up the road to life.

HENRY MILLER   *The Cosmological Eye*   1939

Proceed, then, clear-eyed and laughing. Go to greet Death as a friend.

RUPERT BROOKE   "Second Best"   1905

Under the wide and starry sky,
Dig the grave and let me lie.
Glad did I live and gladly die,
And I lay me down with a will.

This be the verse you grave for me:
Here he lies where he longed to be:
Home is the sailor, home from the sea,
And the hunter home from the hill.

ROBERT LOUIS STEVENSON   "Requiem"   1887

I would prefer to die in a reasonably dry ditch, under the stars.

GEORGE BERNARD SHAW

On the day when death will knock at thy door,
what wilt thou offer to him? I will set before my
guest the full vessel of my life; I will never let him
go with empty hands. All the sweet vintage of all my
autumn days and summer nights, all the earnings
and gleanings of my busy life will I place before him
at the close of my days, when death will knock at
my door.

RABINDRANATH TAGORE   *Gitanjali*   1912

These are the things I have laid down:
Sorrow, doubt and confusion.
These are the things I have taken up:
Labor, love and understanding.
He who hath laid down his armor,
When the sword hath finished his victory,
Letteth his soul forth as a young eagle
In the early morn, with the sun upon its wings,
And the rose kiss of morn upon its crest,
Unfettered of the day,
Freed for the heights.

PATIENCE WORTH   "The Triumph of Death"   1922

Death is no threat to people who are not afraid to die.

LAO TZU   4th Century B.C.

As to you, Death, and your bitter hug of mortality,
it is idle to try to alarm me.

WALT WHITMAN   *Leaves of Grass*   1892

A person who feels he has lived his life the way he
wanted is not afraid.

STANLEY KELEMAN   *Living Your Dying*   1974

All that nature has prescribed must be good; and as
Death is natural to us, it is absurdity to fear it.

SIR RICHARD STEELE   *The Tatler*   1709

What have I to fear?
If their arrows hit,
If their arrows kill,
What is there in that
To cry about?
Others have gone before,
Others will follow.

DAG HAMMARSKJÖLD   *Markings*   1964

If only I could secure a violent death, what a fine
success! I wish to die in my boots; no more Land of
Counterpane for me. To be drowned, to be shot, to
be thrown from my horse—aye, to be hanged,
rather than pass again through that slow dissolution.

ROBERT LOUIS STEVENSON   *Vailima Letters*   1895

What enemy do we now perceive advancing against
us, you whom I ride now, as we stand pawing this
stretch of pavement? It is death. Death is the enemy.
It is death against whom I ride with my spear
couched and my hair flying back like a young
man's.... I strike my spurs into my horse. Against
you I will fling myself, unvanquished and
unyielding, O death!

VIRGINIA WOOLF   *The Waves*   1931

It is better to die on your feet than to live on
your knees.

DOLORES IBARRURI   (speech)   1936

I hope to die at my post, on the street, or in prison.

ROSA LUXEMBURG

(in a letter to Sonia Liebknecht)   1919

I shall die. Where is the terror in this? Have not very many changes taken place in my carnal existence without causing me fear? Why, then, am I afraid of this change, which has not yet taken place and in which there is not only nothing contrary to reason and experience, but which is so intelligible, familiar and natural to me that in the course of my life I have constantly made combinations, in which the death both of animals and men has been accepted by me as a necessary and often as an agreeable condition of life? Where is here the terror?

LEO TOLSTOY   *The Meaning of Life*

If we haven't lived like cowards we are not apt to die like cowards.

AVIS D. CARLSON   *In the Fullness of Time*   1977

Cowards die many times before their death;
The valiant never taste of death but once.

Of all the wonders that I yet have heard
It seems to me most strange that man should fear,
Seeing that death, a necessary end,
Will come when it will.

WILLIAM SHAKESPEARE   *Julius Caesar*

In reply to a query whether he was afraid of death,
Einstein replied: "I feel such solidarity with all living
things that it does not matter to me where the
individual begins and ends."

(ATTRIBUTED)

Perhaps the best cure for the fear of death is to
reflect that life has a beginning as well as an end.
There was a time when you were not: that gives us
no concern. Why then should it trouble us that a
time will come when we shall cease to be? To die is
only to be as we were before we were born.

WILLIAM HAZLITT   *Table Talk*   1821

When I depart, I cast no look behind, since life and
death in cycles come and go. Life follows upon
death. Death is the beginning of life. Who knows

when the end is reached? The life of man results
from convergence of the vital fluid. Its convergence
is life, its dispersion, death. If then life and death are
but consecutive states, what need have I to
complain?

CHUANG TZU   300 B.C.

Serene I fold my hands and wait,
　　Nor care for wind, nor tide, nor sea;
I rave no more 'gainst time or fate,
　　For, lo! my own shall come to me.

I stay my haste, I make delays,
　　For what avails this eager pace?
I stand amid the eternal ways,
　　And what is mine shall know my face.

The stars come nightly to the sky;
　　The tidal wave comes to the sea;
Nor time, nor space, nor deep, nor high,
　　Can keep my own away from me.

JOHN BURROUGHS   "Waiting"   1906

Life is a process of disintegration which is consistently throwing us back into nature. Death on the other hand, is not the entrance into, but rather the end of this process of disintegration. Why do we not rather fear life, in which this is an infinitely more frequent occurrence than in death?

GUSTAV FECHNER   *Life After Death*   1836

Afraid? Of whom am I afraid?
Not death; for who is he?
The porter of my father's lodge
As much abasheth me.

EMILY DICKINSON   *Poems*   1870

Death? Why this fuss about death? Use your imagination. Try to visualize a world without death! Death is the essential condition of life, not an evil.

CHARLOTTE PERKINS GILMAN
Life of Charlotte Perkins Gilman   1935

Do I fear the invisible dark hand of death—
plucking me into the darkness, gathering me

blossom by blossom from the stem of life into the unknown of my afterwards? I fear it only in reverence and with strange satisfaction.

D.H. LAWRENCE

Joy! shipmate—joy!
(Pleas'd to my Soul at death I cry)—
Our life is closed—our life begins;
The long, long anchorage we leave!
The ship is clear at last, she leaps!
She swiftly courses from the shore.
Joy! shipmate—joy!

WALT WHITMAN   *Leaves of Grass*   1892

Here begins the open sea. Here begins the glorious adventure, the only one abreast with human curiosity, the only one that soars as high as its highest longing. Let us accustom ourselves to regard death as a form of life which we do not yet understand; let us learn to look upon it with the same eye that looks upon birth; and soon our mind will be accompanied to the steps of the tomb with the same glad expectation as greets a birth.

MAURICE MAETERLINCK   *Our Eternity*   1913

My delight in death is far, far greater than
The delight of traders at making vast fortunes at sea,
Or the lords of the gods who vaunt their victories in
    battle;
Or of those sages who have entered the rapture of
    perfect absorption.
So just as a traveler who set out on the road when
    the time has come to go,
I will not remain in this world any longer,
But will go to dwell in the stronghold of the great
    bliss of deathlessness.
This, my life, is finished, my karma is exhausted.
What benefit prayers could bring has worn out.
All worldly things are done with.
This life's show is over.
In one instant I will recognize the very essence of
    the manifestation of my being
In the pure, vast realms of the bardo states.
I am close now to taking up my seat in the ground
    of primordial perfection.

THE TIBETAN LONGCHENPAS   *Last Testament*   1400

Mr. Valiant-for-Truth called for his friends and said
"I am going to my Father's, and though with great
difficulty I have got hither, yet now I do not regret

me of all the Trouble I have been at to arrive where I am. My Sword I give to him that shall succeed me in my Pilgrimage, and my Courage and Skill to him that can get it. My Marks and Scars I carry with me, to be witness for me that I have fought his Battle who will now be my Rewarder...." Many accompanied him to the Riverside, into which as he went he said "Death, where is thy Sting?" And as he went deeper, he said, "Grave, where is thy Victory?" Singing, he passed over, and all the Trumpets sounded for him on the other side.

JOHN BUNYAN   *Pilgrim's Progress*   1678

I shall welcome Death as princes do some great ambassadors.

JOHN WEBSTER   *The White Devil*   1608

The overtakelessness of those
Who have accomplished Death,
Majestic is to me beyond
The majesties of Earth.
The soul her "Not At Home"
Inscribes upon the flesh,

And takes her fair aerial gait
Beyond the hope of touch.

<small>EMILY DICKINSON</small>   *Poems*   1890

Farewell, my brethren,
Farewell O earth and sky,
Farewell ye neighboring waters,
My time has ended,
My term has come.

<small>WALT WHITMAN</small>   *Leaves of Grass*   1855

Death is before me today—like the recovery of a sick
    man, like going forth into a garden after illness.
Death is before me today—like the odour of lotus
    flowers, like sitting on the banks of flowing waters.
Death is before me today—like the course of a
    freshet, like the return of a man from the war
    galley to his home.
Death is before me today—like a physician with a
    healing ointment for a man weary with shield and
    sword-work.
Death is before me today—as a man longs to see his
    house, after he has spent many years in captivity.

Death is before me today.
O Friend, your hand in this darkness. Welcome!
(FROM THE EGYPTIAN)

The soul lives after the body dies. The soul passes
through the Great Gate and makes a way in the
darkness to its source. Let this soul pass on.
(FROM THE EGYPTIAN)

DEATH, THE GREAT GOOD

No one knows whether death, which men in their fear apprehend to be the greatest evil, may not be the greatest good.

SOCRATES

Death is, by all odds, the most important and over-shadowing thing that confronts man. Of all the phenomena of nature confronting him, there is nothing else of any great importance.

CLARENCE DARROW   (in a lecture)   1920

It is impossible that anything so natural, so necessary, and so universal as death should ever have been designed by providence as an evil to mankind.

JONATHAN SWIFT   *Thoughts on Religion*   1731

In my youth I received this answer from my father when I asked him what he thought about a future life: he answered, "We may be certain that whatever it may be, no one will be disappointed."

RALPH WALDO EMERSON   "Immortality"   1883

The truest account of heaven is the fairest, and I will accept none which disappoints expectation.

H.D. THOREAU   *Journal*   1852

The thought of death leaves me in perfect peace, for I have a firm conviction that our spirit is a being of indestructible nature. It works from eternity to eternity. It is like the sun, which though it seems to set in our mortal eyes does not really set, but shines on perpetually.

GOETHE   1830

At death we step into a still more free, quite new domain, which is yet not detached from the other, but rather encloses it in a wider circle.

GUSTAV FECHNER   *Life After Death*   1936

There is neither a here nor a beyond, only the great unity.

RAINER MARIA RILKE   *Sonnets to Orpheus*   1942

Perhaps there will be a great awakening; and each will cease to be an Ego but an All, and will know the divinity of Man by seeing, as the veil falls, himself in each and all.

LAFCADIO HEARN   *Letters from the Raven*   1930

For myself, as it happens, almost the only thing I have never doubted is that our sojourn here on earth is part of a larger process.

MALCOLM MUGGERIDGE
"Half In Love With Death"   1970

With garden resurrections every year,
Life after death is not so queer.

AGNES RYAN   *Poems*   1950

I feel and know that death is not the ending, as we thought, but rather the real beginning—and that nothing ever is or can be lost, nor even die, nor soul, nor matter.

WALT WHITMAN   *Democratic Vistas*

I say that the tomb, which closes on the dead, opens the firmament. And that what on earth we call the end, is the commencement.... Death is the portal of life.

VICTOR HUGO

Physical death is one of life's eternal moments and not necessarily a very crucial one.

HUGH I'A. FAUSSET   *Towards Fidelity*   1952

Don't think of death as extinction; such uninspired speculations are simply much too prosaic to be true. Your dull imagination insults the very grandeur and staggering wonder of this universe.... Don't project your callow views upon the universe.

BRIAN SWIMME   *The Universe Is A Green Dragon*   1984

Death is only a larger kind of going abroad.

SAMUEL BUTLER   *Notebooks*   1912

Death is psychologically just as important as birth and life. It is an integral part of life—an extension of existence. Shrinking away from it is something unhealthy and abnormal which robs the second half of life of its purpose. Not to want the climax of our life is not to see through to the end. Becoming and passing away are the same curve.

CARL JUNG   1961

Death is our eternal companion. It is always at our left, at an arm's length.... Ask death's advice and drop the cursed pettiness that belongs to men that live their lives as if death will never tap them.... Feel its presence around you.

CARLOS CASTANEDA   *Journey to Ixtlan*   1972

This presence I have talked about will follow me across the frontier, too; whatever "I" shall be, "I" shall need its company because the laws of causation will not cease with the death of my body.

LIONEL BLUE   *A Back Door to Heaven*   1979

Death is an essential part of the successful functioning of life.... New organisms cannot perform their role properly unless the old ones are removed from the scene after they have performed their function in producing the new. In short, the death of the individual is essential to the life of the species.

ISAAC ASIMOV   *A Choice of Catastrophes*   1980

Death is the transfiguration of the living. Corpses are but the dead leaves of the Tree of Life which will still have all its leaves in the Spring.

ELIPHAS LEVY   *Death*   1881

Every part of nature teaches that the passing away of one life is the making of room for another. The oak dies down to the ground, leaving within its rind a rich virgin mold, which will impart a vigorous life to an infant forest.

HENRY DAVID THOREAU   *Journal*   1837

When any living thing has come to the end of its cycle, we accept that end as natural. When that intangible cycle has run its course it is a natural and not unhappy thing that a life comes to its end.

RACHEL CARSON   (in a letter to a friend)   1963

Death is happening each moment in millions of ways around the world. Existence lives through death; existence renews itself through death. Death is the greatest mystery—more mysterious than life, because life is only a pilgrimage toward death.

Death is the culmination of life, the ultimate blossoming of life. In death the whole of life is summed up; in death you arrive.

BHAGAWAN RAJNEESH   *The Revolution*   1979

Death is the regular, indispensable condition of the replacement of one individual by another along a phylatic stem. Death is the essential lever in the mechanism and upsurge of life.

TEILHARD DE CHARDIN   *The Phenomenon of Man*   1959

Whatever is organic is mortal. And the death of the organism is the end of organic life. But it is not necessarily the end of individual personality, nor even of personal consciousness.

JOHN MACMURRAY   *Reason and Emotion*   1938

You do not cease to exist at death. That is only illusion. You go through the doorway of death alive and there is no altering of the consciousness. It is not a strange land you go to but a land of living reality where the growth process is a continuation.... Death is only a passage through, a time of release. The fear of death is the fear of letting go.... Why would it be supposed that one's creative ability ceases at the moment consciousness leaves the physical? The instant that the Self releases from the human body there is light, there is peace, there is freedom, there is home.

PAT RODEGAST and JUDITH STANTON

Emmanuel's Book   1985

Nobody knows that death stays the development of the individual. It stays our perception of it; but so does distance, absence or even sleep. Birth gives to each of us much; death may give more, in the way of subtler senses to behold colours we cannot now see; to catch sounds which we do not now hear; and to be aware of bodies and objects impalpable at present to us, but perfectly real.

SIR EDWIN ARNOLD   *Death And Afterwards*   1901

... To lose the earth you know, for greater knowing; to lose the life you have, for greater life; to leave the friends you loved, for greater loving; to find a land more kind than home, more large than

earth—whereon the pillars of this earth are
founded, toward which the conscience of the world
is tending....

THOMAS WOLFE
"Credo" in *You Can't Go Home Again*   1934

Dear lovely Death
That taketh all things under wing—
Never to kill—
Only to change
Into some other thing.
This suffering flesh,
To make it neither more or less,
But not again the same—
Dear lovely Death,
Change is thy other name.

LANGSTON HUGHES   1945

"Could one," he asked himself, "ever come to
regard death as a delicious resting from life, an
appointed goal?"

A.C. BENSON   *Beside Still Waters*   1907

If death could be seen as a beautiful clear lake, refreshing and bouyant, then when a consciousness moves towards its exit from a body there would be that delightful plunge and it would simply swim away.

PAT RODEGAST and JUDITH STANTON
Emmanuel's Book   1987

We are spirits. That bodies should be lent us while they afford us pleasure, assist us in acquiring knowledge or in doing good to our fellow-creatures, is a kind of benevolent act of God. When they become unfit for these purposes and afford us pain instead of pleasure, instead of an aid become an encumbrance and answer none of these intentions for which they were given, it is equally kind and benevolent that a way is provided by which we get rid of them. Death is that way.

BENJAMIN FRANKLIN
(letter after the death of his brother)   1756

The unending death-roll of all creatures, including ourselves, is the essential complement to the unceasing renewal of life.

J. E. LOVELOCK   *Gaia*   1987

What we commonly call death in man is not death at all, but only a change of the energy of life into another form, where it may still exist, albeit in different circumstances and operating through and upon different kinds of instrumentality.... Life, being a form of force, or energy, of something greater than mere physical force or energy, can never wholly cease to be. Therefore "death" is not the end of life, but only a change whereby it continues actively in another form.

JON P. HALSEY   *The Evidence for Immortality*   1931

Life after death is made by aspirations and spiritual development. According to the growth of each, so is his life after death. It is the complement of his life here. All unsatisfied spiritual longings, all desires for a higher life, all aspiration and dreams of noble things come to flower in the spiritual life, and the soul has its day, for life on earth is its night.

H.P. BLAVATSKY   *Theosophical Journal*   April 1900

There is no death—only changes in modes of consciousness.

F.W.H. MYERS

Human Personality & Its Survival of Bodily Death   1903

Life and death are not two opposed forces; they are simply two ways of looking at the same force, for the movement of change is as much the builder as the destroyer.

ALAN WATTS   *The Wisdom of Insecurity*   1951

There are two bodies—the rudimental and the complete, corresponding with the two conditions of the worm and the butterfly. What we call "death" is but the painful metamorphosis. Our present incarnation is progressive, preparatory, temporary. Our future is perfected, ultimate, immortal. The ultimate life is the full design.

EDGAR ALLEN POE   *Mesmeric Revelations*   1844

Turn which way we will, we find no "killing principle" in Nature, only a vitalising and sustaining one. Throughout its extent, Nature is life, in all forms and modifications—one vast and infinite life, subject no doubt to the extinction of particular phenomena, but never to absolute total death, even in its weakest and least of things. Anything that looks like death is a token and certificate of life being about to start anew. Death and life are but the struggle of life itself to attain a higher form.

C.H. BJERRAGAARD   *The Great Mother*   1913

When the seed bursts, the plant then suddenly spreads asunder. At that instant it feels that it is being dissolved, after lying so long narrowly folded in the seed. On the contrary, it gains a new world.... Birth must seem to the new-born babe what death seems to us—the annihilation of all the conditions which had hitherto made life possible in the womb of its mother, but proved to be its emergence into a wider life.

GUSTAVE FECHNER   *Life After Death*   1936

Nothing is ever really lost, or can be lost,
No birth, identity, form—no object of the world.
Nor life, nor force, nor any visible thing;
Appearance must not foil, nor shifted sphere
    confuse thy brain.
Ample are time and space—ample the fields of
    Nature.
The body, sluggish, aged, cold—the embers left
    from earlier fires,

The light in the eye grown dim, shall duly flame
    again;
The sun now low in the west rises for mornings and
    for noons continual;
To frozen clods ever the spring's invisible law
    returns,
With grass and flowers and summer fruits and corn.

WALT WHITMAN   *Leaves of Grass*   1884

We are asked to believe that man, the living,
thinking, reasoning entity, the indwelling deity of
nature's crowning masterpiece, will evacuate his
casket and be no more. Would the principle of
continuity which exists even for the so-called
inorganic matter, for a floating stone, be denied to
the spirit, whose attributes are consciousness,
memory, mind, and love? Really, the very idea is
preposterous.

H.P. BLAVATSKY   *Isis Unveiled*   1877

Can the world which has produced such worth now
dash it to oblivion? It is a cry against wastefulness in
the universe. Thus the idea of survival arises far

more as a claim of rightness than a personal wish. It is conceived as an obligation of the cosmos to itself—a right we claim to affection and to justice in the world—to purpose in the universe.

HELEN HOWELL NEAL   *The Universe and You*   1954

If men believe that the universe has a unity and a dominating purpose, or makes on the whole some sort of sense, they are prone to conclude that the minds of men must be able somehow to carry on their adventure.

WILLIAM ERNEST HOCKING
The Meaning of Immortality   1957

The assumption that nothing preceded birth or follows death is largely taken for granted in the West.... Such an assertion rests on the blind assumption, in its own way an act of faith, that life, of all things in the universe, operates in a vacuum. It asks us to believe that this one phenomenon, the invigoration of supposedly inert matter, springs out of nowhere and just as miraculously disappears without a trace.

PHILIP KAPLEAU   *The Wheel of Death*   1971

Why cheat ourselves with words so vague as life and death? What is the difference? At most, the entrance in and the departure from one scene in our wide career. How many scenes are left to us! We do but hasten our journey, not close it.

EDWARD BULWER-LYTTON   *Godolphin*   1870

For life and death are one, even as the river and the sea are one.

KAHLIL GIBRAN   *The Prophet*   1934

The world of eternity is the divine bosom onto which we shall all go after the death of the vegetated body.

WILLIAM BLAKE

To see through the eyes of the mountain eagle, the view of realization, is to look down on a landscape in which the boundaries that we imagined existed between life and death shade into each other and dissolve.... What we, in our ignorance, call "life," and what we, in our ignorance, call "death," are merely different aspects of that wholeness and movement.

SOGYAL RINPOCHE

The Tibetan Book of Living and Dying   1992

Death is much simpler than birth; it is merely a continuation. Birth is the mystery, not death.

STEWART EDWARD WHITE

The Unobstructed Universe   1940

Nothing is more creative than death, since it is the whole secret of life. Death is the unknown in which all of us lived before birth.

ALAN WATTS   *The Wisdom of Insecurity*   1951

Life and death are but phases of the same thing, the reverse and obverse of the same coin. Death is as necessary for man's growth as life itself.

MOHANDAS GANDHI   1920

That which has been born must die. The two are one: birth and death are one event which happens to a being, but which is cleft in twain by a little fissure we call life.

SIR EDWIN ARNOLD   *Death and Afterwards*   1901

It didn't begin here and it won't end here.

MABEL TELFORD   *Strings from a Broken Lute*   1970

Death is the end of a stage, not the end of the journey. The road stretches on beyond our comprehension.

SIR OLIVER LODGE   *Life And Death*   1915

There is no death of anyone but only in appearance, even as there is no birth save only in seeming. The change from being to becoming seems to be birth, and the change from becoming to being seems to be death, but in reality no one is ever born, nor does anyone ever die. It is simply being visible and then invisible.

APOLLONIUS OF TYANA   (letter to Valerius)   70 A.D.

That which dies in a man is only his five senses.
That which continues to exist, beyond his senses, is
immense, unimaginable, sublime.

ANTON CHEKHOV   *Notebook*   1904

This is birth, not death; freedom after bondage.
Gain, not loss; light following after shadow.

MARGARET CAMERON   *The Seven Purposes*   1918

I know that the day will come when my sight of this
earth shall be lost, and life will take its leave in
silence, drawing the last curtain over my eyes. Yet
stars will watch at night, and morning rise as before
and hours heave like sea waves casting up pleasures
and pains. When I think of this end of my moments,
the barrier of the moments breaks and I see by the
light of death thy world with its careless treasures.
Rare is its lowliest seat, rare is its meanest of lives.

RABINDRANATH TAGORE   *Gitanjali*   1912

The tomb is not a blind alley; it is an open
thoroughfare. It is hardly above its foundation. I

would gladly see it mounting forever. The thirst for
infinity proves infinity.

VICTOR HUGO   1880

This body is mortal, forever in the clutch of death.
But within it resides the Self, immortal, and
without form. Riding above physical consciousness,
knowing the Self as distinct from the sense-organs
and the mind, knowing Him in His true light, one
rejoices and is free.

CHANDOGYA UPANISHAD

It is the spirit that tires of its earthly habitation, that
wearies of the cramping limitations of the house of
flesh; and in proportion as it struggles to draw itself
away, the vital forces of the body are weakened, the
subconscious that guides its myriad functions is
affected and disturbed, until at last the final
separation takes place, and the body is cast off, its
purpose accomplished—even as the serpent casts
off its skin.

EVA MARTIN   *The Secret of A Star*   1913

Death is a dialogue between
The spirit and the dust.
"Dissolve," says Death. The Spirit, "Sir,
I have another Trust."
Death doubts it, argues from the ground.
The Spirit turns away,
Just laying off, for evidence,
An overcoat of clay.

EMILY DICKINSON   *Poems*   1890

You simply divest yourself of physical
paraphernalia, tune into different fields, and react to
other sets of assumptions.

JANE ROBERTS   *Seth Speaks*   1972

The fever called "living" is conquered at last.

EDGAR ALLEN POE   "For Annie"   1844

The soothing sanity and blitheness of completion,
The pomp and hurried contest-glare and rush are
    done.
Now triumph! transformation! jubilate!

WALT WHITMAN   *Leaves of Grass*   1892

Death, so called, is but old matter dressed
In some new figure, and a varied vest.
Thus all things are but altered, nothing dies;
Here and there the unbodied spirit flies.
The form is only changed, the wax is still the same.
Death, so called, can but the form deface;
The immortal soul flies out in empty space
To seek her fortune in some other place.

OVID   10 A.D.

Death for a philosopher is the final fulfillment,
much to be desired, because it opens the door to
true knowledge. The soul, freed from its bonds to
the body, at last achieves undimmed and celestial
vision.

SOCRATES, ON HIS LAST DAY

Death is the active force; life is the arena....
Without a clear view of death, there is no order, no
sobriety, no beauty.

CARLOS CASTANEDA   *The Power of Silence*   1987

How cordial is the mystery!
  The hospitable Pall.
A "this way" beckons spaciously—
  A Miracle for all!

EMILY DICKINSON   *Poems*   1890

Earth and death seem to be respectively the Great
Exile and the Great Returning Home.

RAYNOR JOHNSON   *The Imprisoned Splendour*   1913

The night kisses the fading day, whispering to his
ear, "I am death, your mother. I am to give you
fresh birth."

RABINDRANATH TAGORE   *Stray Birds*   1917

Does the road wind uphill all the way?
  Yes, to the very end.
Will the day's journey take the whole long day?
  From morn tonight, my friend.
But is there for the night a resting-place?
  A roof for when the slow dark hours begin.
May not the darkness hide it from my face?
  You cannot miss that inn.

Shall I meet other wayfarers at night?
    Those who have gone before.
Then must I knock, or call when just in sight?
    They will not keep you standing at that door.
Shall I find comfort, travel-sore and weak?
    Of labor you shall find the sum.
Will there be beds for me and all who seek?
    Yes, beds for all who come.

CHRISTINA ROSSETTI   *Poems*   1896

Look upon death as a going home.

CHINESE PROVERB

We shall all meet again, when we have arrived.

LEO TOLSTOY   (attributed)

On this wondrous sea
Sailing silently,
Ho! Pilot, ho!
Knowest thou the shore
Where no breakers roar—
Where the storm is o'er?

In the peaceful west
Many the sails at rest—
The anchors fast—
Thither I pilot thee—
Land! Ho! Eternity!
Ashore at last!

EMILY DICKINSON   *Poems*   1890

I cannot think of death as more than the going out
of one room into another.

WILLIAM BLAKE   1826

Surely death acquires a new and deeper significance
when we regard it no longer as a single and
unexplained break in an unending life, but as a part
of the continuously recurring rhythm of progress—
as inevitable, as natural and as benevolent as sleep.

J. McTAGGART   *Some Dogmas of Religion*

You should think the death of your body a no
greater break in your continuity of living in this
world than is the retiring for a night's sleep in your
present body.

HAROLD W. PERCIVAL   *Thinking and Destiny*   1946

Death is as natural and necessary as birth, and it is no more mysterious. Death is only change, a necessary incident of the continuous life of the world. Bad as is our social state, it is easy to see that if death did not cut off the unfit, the world would be filled with nothing but misery. When the house of the flesh becomes so worn or so diseased as to be beyond repair, life pulls it down and rebuilds afresh: that is what we call death.

BOLTON HALL   *The Halo of Grief*   1919

It may be that personal immortality is indeed a myth. But individual immortality is one of the deepest truths of life. For the personality, made up of mental and physical characteristics of a person, belongs to the changing world of time, whereas the individuality consists of those enduring qualities which belong to the spirit of man and of which the personality or mask-self is only the outer garment.

LAURENCE J. BENDIT   *This World and That*   1950

Perhaps what dies is only the dear trivial familiar self of each. Perhaps in our annihilation some vital and eternal thing does break wing, fly free. Whether

we are annihilated or attain in some strange way
eternal life, to have lived and loved is good.

Olaf Stapledon   *Death Into Life*   1946

We cannot suppose that death is the end of any
adventure except that of the body.... There will be
things yet to be done, and the stuff that we work in
will be the utterly familiar and still mysterious and
exciting stuff of ourselves.

Mary Austin   *Experiences Facing Death*   1931

If it is true that we survive death it is inherent in the
nature of life itself, and has nothing to do with any
religion or philosophy.... Instinctively I feel that
death does not close the doors of perception and
feeling. It does not write "finis" to the book of life.

Dr. Lyle Telford
(in a letter to Scott Nearing)   1969

The Body of B. Franklin, Printer,
Like the Cover of an Old Book,
Its Contents Torn Out
And Stripped of its Lettering and Gilding,

Lies Here Food for Worms.
But the Work shall not be Lost,
For it will, as he believed, appear Once More
In a New and more Elegant Edition
Revised and Corrected by the Author.

BENJAMIN FRANKLIN'S EPITAPH, WHICH HE WROTE AT 22

Who that has mourned and not failed of the promised comfort can ever question the living fact of immortality? The soul has a body, and well does that soul know when this body has served its purpose. And well does that soul do to lay it aside in high austerity, taking it off like a stained garment.

LUCIEN PRICE   *Litany for All Souls*   1924

Unborn, eternal, the soul is not slain, though the body is slain. If the slayer thinks to slay it, if the slain thinks it is slain, it slays not nor is slain. Thinking of the soul as unbodily among bodies, firm among unfirm things, the wise man casts off all grief.

KATHA UPANISHAD

This world is not conclusion;
    A sequel stands beyond,
Invisible, as music,
    But positive, as sound.
It beckons and it baffles;
    Philosophies don't know,
And through a riddle, at the last,
    Sagacity must go.
To guess it puzzles scholars;
    To gain it, men have shown
Contempt of generations,
    And crucifixion known.

EMILY DICKINSON   *Poems*   1890

Death is the final stage of growth in this life. There is no total death. Only the body dies. The self or spirit, or whatever you may wish to label it, is eternal.

ELISABETH KÜBLER-ROSS
Death: The Final Stage of Growth   1975

The more I observe and study things, the more convinced I become that sorrow over separation and death is perhaps the greatest delusion. To realise that it is a delusion is to become free. There is no death, no separation of the substance. And yet the tragedy of it is that though we love friends for the substance we recognize in them, we deplore the destruction of the insubstantial part that covers the substance only for the time being. Whereas real friendship should be used to reach the whole through the fragment.

MOHANDAS GANDHI   *Letters to a Disciple*   1950

To die is to begin to live. It is to end an old, stale, weary work and to commence a new and a better. 'Tis to leave deceitful knaves, for the society of gods and goodness.   Why should I grieve or vex for being sent to them I ever loved best?

SOPHOCLES, AT HIS EXECUTION

The mind of the survivor is mean; it sees the loss, it does not always feel the deliverance.

GRAHAM BALFOUR

The Life of Robert Louis Stevenson   1901

The very delusion of delusions is the idea of death as loss. When all the stars of the visible night shall have burnt themselves, these atoms will doubtless again take part in the orbing of Mind and will tremble again in thoughts, emotions, memories in all the joys and pains of lives still to be lived in worlds still to be evolved.

LAFCADIO HEARN   *Kotto*   1900

The fact is that so far from mourning death you ought to honour it and reverence it.

APOLLONIUS OF TYANA   (letter to Valerius)   70 A.D.

The major problem of our time is the decay of the belief in personal immortality.

GEORGE ORWELL
Looking Back on the Spanish War   1945

Like everybody else, I am incapable of conceiving infinity; and yet I do not accept finity.

SIMONE DE BEAUVOIR   *Old Age*   1972

In every unbeliever's heart there is an uneasy feeling that, after all, he may awake after death and find himself immortal.

H. L. MENCKEN   *A Mencken Christomathy*   1949

It is to a thinking being quite impossible to think himself non-existent, ceasing to think and live; so far does every one carry in himself the proof of immortality, and quite spontaneously.

GOETHE   1830

I am standing on the seashore. A ship at my side spreads her white sails to the morning breeze and starts for the blue ocean. She is an object of beauty and strength. I stand and watch her until at length she is only a ribbon of white cloud just where the sea and sky come to mingle with each other. There! She is gone! But someone at my side says "Gone where?" From our sight, that is all. She is just as large in mast and hull and spar as when she left our side, and just as able to bear her load of living freight to the place of destination. Her diminished size is in us, not in her. Just at the moment when you say "There! She is gone!" other voices are ready to take up the glad shout: "There she comes!" And that is what we call dying.

We cannot say that death is not a good. We do not know whether the grave is the end of this life, or the door of another, or whether the night here is not somewhere else a dawn.

ROBERT G. INGERSOLL   *Why I am an Agnostic*   1890

Death is the dissolving of a partnership, the partners to which survive and go elsewhere. It is the corruption and breaking up of that society which we have called Ourself. The corporation is at an end, both its soul and body cease as a whole, but the immortal constituents do not cease and never will.

SAMUEL BUTLER   *Notebook*   1870

The extraordinary adventure of the world will have ended in the bosom of a tranquil ocean, of which, however, each drop will still be conscious of being itself.

TEILHARD DE CHARDIN   *Mon Univers*   1924

Death is the supreme form of life.... We must accept our own death, and the deaths of others, as a natural part of life.

MARGUERITE YOURCENAR   *With Open Eyes*   1980

Death is not putting out the light. It is only extinguishing a lamp because the day has come.

RABINDRANATH TAGORE

We are not snuffed out at death but absorbed into a greater flame.

ANNE MORROW LINDBERGH
Hours of Gold, Hours of Lead   1973

Death! Think of the infinity of space and time. No haste; no pressure. All scintillating peace and wonder.

PIETRO FERRUCHI   *What We May Be*   1982

The light which puts out our eyes is darkness to us. Only that day dawns to which we are awake. There is more day to dawn. The sun is but a morning star.

HENRY DAVID THOREAU   *Walden*   1854

I am a firm believer in the personal survival of the real individual after the death of the mortal body which they happen to be inhabiting.

RALPH HOLLAND   "A Voice from the Gallery"   1950

Is man immortal?" the Buddha was asked. "Not the man you know," was the reply.

If we call life a journey, and death the inn we reach at last in the evening when it is over; that, too, I feel will be only as brief a stopping-place as any other inn would be. Our experience here is so scanty and shallow—nothing more than the moment of the continual present. Surely that must go on, even if one does call it eternity. And so we shall all have to begin again.

WALTER DE LA MARE   *The Return*   1910

Edison, asked by reporters whether he believed in survival after death replied, "The only survival I can conceive is to start a new life cycle again."

From death onwards, the adventure of the universe becomes our adventure. Let us not, therefore, say to ourselves "What can it matter, we shall not be there." We shall be there always, because everything will be there.

MAURICE MAETERLINCK   *Our Eternity*   1913

Never the Spirit was born—
The Spirit shall cease to be, never.
Never was time it was not—
End and beginning are dreams.
Birthless and deathless and changeless
Abideth the Spirit forever.
Death doth not touch it at all
Dead though the house of it seems.

THE BHAGAVAD GITA   500 B.C.

Many things, beyond a doubt, remain to be said which others will say with greater force and brilliance. But we need have no hope that one will utter on this earth the word that shall put an end to our uncertainties. It is very probable, on the contrary, that no one in this world, nor perhaps in the next, will discover the great secret of the universe. Behold us then before the mystery of the cosmic consciousness.

MAURICE MAETERLINCK   *Our Eternity*   1913

INDEX

Upon her death in 1995, Helen Nearing entrusted her estate to The Trust for Public Land (TPL), a national nonprofit organization in the United States committed to conserving land for people. TPL is serving as steward to Forest Farm, Scott and Helen Nearing's home, and their intellectual assets until a new nonprofit organization, The Good Life Center, is able to operate independently.

The Good Life Center will carry on the Nearing legacy, continuing to teach how to create a lifestyle that integrates the values of simple living, ecological respect, and social justice. Through educational programs, publications, and the preservation of Forest Farm as a place for inspiration, The Good Life Center will encourage others to pursue their own versions of "the good life," in order to build a just and sustainable society. If you have any questions or would like to be more involved, please call the Trust for Public Land at 617-367-6200, fax at 617-367-1616, or write to The Good Life Center, Box 11, Harborside, ME 04642.